DK EYEWITNESS TRAVEL

W9-AEG-099

TOP 10
CUBA

WITHDRAWN
BY
WILLIAMSBURG REGIONAL LIBRARY
CHRISTOPHER P. BAKER

Penguin
Random
House

Top 10 Cuba Highlights

The Top 10 of Everything

CONTENTS

Cuba
Area by Area

Streetsmart

Within each Top 10 list in this book, no hierarchy of quality or popularity is implied. All 10 are, in the editor's opinion, of roughly equal merit.
  Throughout this book, floors are referred to in accordance with American usage; i.e., the "first floor" is at ground level.

Front cover and spine Former Summer Palace, Palacio del Valle at Punta Gorda in Cienfuegos
Back cover Trinidad backed by the Sierra del Escambray mountains
Title page Beach with palm trees on Cayo Levisa Island

The information in this DK Eyewitness Top 10 Travel Guide is checked regularly. Every effort has been made to ensure that this book is as up-to-date as possible at the time of going to press. Some details, however, such as telephone numbers, opening hours, prices, gallery hanging arrangements, and travel information, are liable to change. The publishers cannot accept responsibility for any consequences arising from the use of this book, nor for any material on third party websites, and cannot guarantee that any website address in this book will be a suitable source of travel information. We value the views and suggestions of our readers very highly. Please write to: Publisher, DK Eyewitness Travel Guides, Dorling Kindersley, 80 Strand, London WC2R 0RL, UK, or email travelguides@dk.com

Welcome to
Cuba

From high-kicking showgirls at the Tropicana cabaret to murals of Che Guevara, sensuality and socialism rub shoulders as defining aspects of Cuba. Add the world's best cigars, plus classic cars cruising cities frozen in the 1950s, and it's no wonder this Caribbean island is a hot destination. With Eyewitness Top 10 Cuba, it's yours to explore.

Havana – the irrepressible capital city – awes us with its stunning architecture and sense of being a yesteryear Hollywood stage set. Walking the cobbled colonial streets of **La Habana Vieja** is a journey back through the centuries, while **Vedado** recalls the wealth of a glittering pre-revolutionary heyday. Chock-full of outstanding museums, art galleries, and lively bars where Ernest Hemingway drank his mojitos and daiquiris, Havana is a world-class city throbbing to the rhythms of rumba and salsa.

Cuba is a marvelously diverse island, from the stunningly beautiful **Valle de Viñales**, where oxen plough tobacco fields, to the gorgeous beaches of **Cayo Coco**. Well-preserved colonial-era cities such as **Trinidad** and **Camagüey** – both UNESCO World Heritage Sites – echo the footsteps of *conquistadores*. In the east, **Santiago de Cuba** is known for its iconic revolutionary sites and a culture that owes much to its predominantly African heritage. Beyond the forest-clad **Sierra Maestra** lies charming **Baracoa**, founded in 1511 and boasting a jaw-dropping setting surrounded by mountains.

Whether you're planning a week's visit or a longer stay, our Top 10 guide reveals the best of everything that Cuba can offer, from **María la Gorda** in the west to **Punta Maisí** in the east. You will find tips throughout, from seeking out what's free to finding the best private restaurants, plus five easy-to-follow itineraries designed to tie together a slew of best sights in a short space of time. Add inspiring photography and detailed maps, and you've got the essential pocket-sized travel companion. **Enjoy the book, and enjoy Cuba.**

Clockwise from top: **Playa Ancón; Gran Teatro, Havana; divers in María la Gorda; street in Trinidad; Cuban cigars; Ford Fairline car; musicians at La Bodeguita del Medio, Havana**

Exploring Cuba

Cuba boasts a remarkable capital city, gorgeous beaches, and exquisite colonial towns. Whether you simply want to immerse yourself in Havana or go farther afield, these two- and seven-day itineraries will help you make the most of this fascinating country.

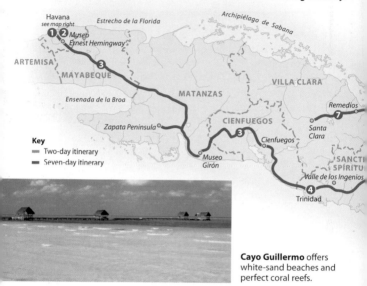

Cayo Guillermo offers white-sand beaches and perfect coral reefs.

Two Days in Havana

Day ❶
MORNING
Hop aboard the **Havana BusTour** *(see p120)* and enjoy an overview sightseeing tour of the entire city. You can alight at any sight you wish to visit; another bus will be along soon, and it's all covered by one all-day ticket.
AFTERNOON
Visit the Modernist Palace of Fine Arts, part of the **Museo Nacional de Bellas Artes** *(see p74)* for its remarkable collection of Cuban art, and **Museo de la Revolución** *(see p75)*, for a profile on the Revolution. Explore **Parque Central** *(see p75)* and walk **Paseo de Martí** *(see p76)*. End the day with a sunset stroll along the **Malecón** *(see p76)*.

Day ❷
MORNING
Explore the quaint colonial plazas of **La Habana Vieja** *(see pp12–13)*, starting with **Plaza de Armas** *(see p72)* and the **Catedral de La Habana** *(see p73)*.
AFTERNOON
Wander along **Calle Mercaderes** *(see p74)* to reach **Plaza Vieja** *(see p73)*. Charming Calle Brasil then connects you to **Plaza de San Francisco** *(see p74)*, with its magnificent basilica.

Seven Days in Cuba

Days ❶ and ❷
Follow the two-day Havana itinerary.

Day ❸
Visit the **Museo Ernest Hemingway** *(see p76)*, then head east via the **Zapata Peninsula** *(see pp18–19)*,

Trinidad is a pretty town where cobbled streets are lined with pastel-colored buildings.

Catedral de La Habana, a gorgeous Baroque edifice, is set in Old Havana.

stopping for lunch before calling at **Museo Girón** (see p19) for a history lesson on the Bay of Pigs invasion (see p41). Travel to the port city of **Cienfuegos** (see p94) and admire the buildings around Plaza Martí before dinner at the astonishing **Palacio del Valle** (see p99).

Day ❹
Drive to **Trinidad** (see pp20–21) to immerse yourself in its delightful colonial mystique as you wander around Plaza Mayor. After lunch, continue exploring Trinidad's cobbled streets. End your day by cooling off at **Playa Ancón** (see pp104–5).

Day ❺
Journey via the scenic **Valle de los Ingenios** (see p103) and follow the Carretera Central to the UNESCO World Heritage city of **Camagüey**

(see pp26–7). Admire the city's recently spruced up historic center, being sure to include charming Plaza del Carmen.

Day ❻
Start early and head across the **Pedraplén** (see p25) to the **Jardines del Rey** (see pp24–5). Laze on your choice of glorious beaches and swim in the warm turquoise sea at **Playa de los Flamencos** or on the island of **Cayo Guillermo** (see p24).

Day ❼
Head west to **Remedios** (see p95) to savor its colonial ambience, then continue to **Santa Clara** (see p94). View the **Monumento del Che** (see p39), beneath which the remains of revolutionary hero Ernesto "Che" Guevara (see p41) are interred, before returning to Havana.

Top 10 Cuba Highlights

Catedral de La Habana, Havana

TOP 10 Cuba Highlights

Cuba is a land of incredible beauty and amazing contrasts, from white-sand beaches and azure seas to lush valleys and cloud-draped mountains. It is set in a time warp of colonial buildings and pre-revolutionary cars, and its vivacious populace is a blend of Spanish, African, Chinese, and Russian peoples.

1 La Habana Vieja, Havana

Colonial castles, palaces, and cobbled plazas recall the days when Old Havana was the New World's richest city (see pp12–13).

2 The Modern City, Havana

This throbbing metropolis offers museums, parks, beaches, 1950s hotels and nightclubs, and stunning examples of architecture from Beaux Arts to *modernismo* (see pp14–15).

La Habana Vieja
The Modern City 2 1
Cordillera de Guaniguanico 3
Pinar del Río
Isabel Rubio
Candelaria
Guanajay
Golfo de Batabanó
Batabanó
Matanzas
Jovellanos
Jagüey Grande
Zapata Peninsula 4
Varadero
Cárdenas
Colón
Cienfuegos
Santa Clara
Archipiélago
Sagu la Gran
Trinidad 5
Archipiélago de los Canarreos
Isla de la Juventud

3 Cordillera de Guaniguanico

A few hours west of Havana, these mountains are known for their dramatic rock formations and spectacular caves (see pp16–17).

4 Zapata Peninsula

This vast swampland and park protects many endemic bird species, and two museums recall the Bay of Pigs invasion of 1961 (see pp18–19).

5 Trinidad

Colorful Trinidad boasts a breeze-swept hillside setting. This lovely UNESCO World Heritage Site is Cuba's most complete colonial city (see pp20–21).

Jardines del Rey ⑥

Stretching 275 miles (442 km) along Cuba's northern coastline, this chain of offshore islands and cays is lined with stunning beaches *(see pp24–5)*.

⑦ Camagüey

The colonial buildings of Camagüey were made a World Heritage Site in 2008, and the city is slowly being restored. It is awash with imposing churches looming over cobbled plazas *(see pp26–7)*.

Holguín ⑧

This provincial capital has played a key role in Cuban history. Its plazas are lined with museums and cultural centers. Castro's birthplace and a beach resort are two nearby attractions *(see pp28–9)*.

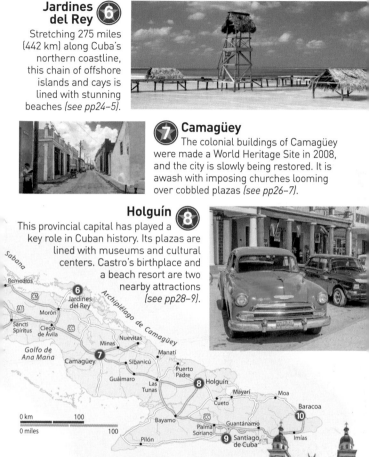

Santiago de Cuba ⑨

Santiago de Cuba exudes a mystique influenced by its French and Afro-Caribbean links. It is home to Cuba's oldest building, a fine cathedral, plus sites and monuments relating to the Revolution *(see pp30–31)*.

Baracoa ⑩

Cuba's first city, founded in 1511, Baracoa enjoys a stupendous bay-side setting backed by rainforest-clad mountains *(see pp32–3)*.

TOP 10 ⭐ La Habana Vieja, Havana

With almost 1,000 buildings of historic importance, this intimate quarter is perhaps the largest and most complete colonial complex in the Americas. Like a peopled museum full of animated street life, Old Havana boasts an astonishing wealth of castles, churches, convents, palaces, and other important buildings spanning five centuries and subject to an ongoing restoration program. Easily walkable, the cobbled plazas and the narrow streets of La Habana Vieja exude charm.

Catedral de La Habana ③

Dominating a cobbled plaza, this cathedral **(right)** is graced by an exquisite Baroque facade with asymmetrical bell towers. The restored interior features fine murals.

④ Calle Mercaderes

This cobbled street links Calle Obispo to Plaza Vieja. Lined with tiny museums, boutiques, colonial mansions, and other attractions, it offers hours of exploration *(see p74)*.

① Palacio de los Capitanes Generales

This former governor's palace **(above)** houses the City Museum. Displays of colonial treasures in lavishly decorated hallways and chambers recall the height of Spanish power.

⑤ Museo Nacional de Bellas Artes

The fine arts museum is housed in two buildings and displays both an international collection and Cuban art **(right)** *(see p74)*.

② Plaza de San Francisco

This harborfront plaza is dominated by the Basílica Menor de San Francisco de Asís, which holds a museum and is a venue for concerts.

⑥ Plaza Vieja

The fountain at the heart of Old Havana's largest plaza **(left)** is an exact replica of the 17th-century original. Sites here include a brew-pub, a boutique, and intimate museums and galleries *(see p73)*.

9 Calle Obispo

This pedestrian-only thoroughfare is lined with book shops, eclectic stores **(left)**, art galleries, music bars, cafés, and a coin museum.

THE CITY WALLS

Havana's fortified city walls were completed in 1697 and encircled the original colonial city. The 30-ft- (9-m-) high wall was protected by nine bastions and a moat. However, by the early 19th century the city was bursting at the seams. This rapid expansion led to the eventual tearing down of the wall in 1863. Today only fragments of the original wall remain.

10 Parque Histórico-Militar Morro-Cabaña

Completed in 1774 as the largest fortress in the Americas, the Cabaña fortress offers dramatic views across the harbor to La Habana Vieja. The Morro castle nearby has a museum on Columbus' voyages.

7 Plaza de Armas

La Habana Vieja's largest cobbled square – the seat of the Spanish government – is the site of the city's first castle, the governor's mansion, and the natural history museum (see p72).

8 Museo de la Revolución

This vast museum in the former Presidential Palace has a whole section dedicated to Che Guevara (see p75).

ᴛᴏᴘ10 ⭐ The Modern City, Havana

Beyond La Habana Vieja, this lively, colorful metropolis of two million people radiates inland from the harbor and coastline like a Spanish fan, emerging from compact 19th-century *barrios* into more spacious 20th-century *municipios* and post-revolutionary suburbs. Apartment blocks give way to once-noble, upper-class districts full of Beaux Arts, Art Deco, and Modernist mansions, while concrete office blocks, government buildings, and hotels from the 1950s give a retro feel.

1 Universidad de La Habana

Havana University has a neo-colonial facade reached via a vast staircase. Its museums **(above)** showcase Cuba's flora, fauna, and pre-Columbian cultures.

2 Capitolio

A replica of Washington D.C.'s Capitol **(below)**, this newly restored Neo-Classical structure is intended once again to be a congressional building. All points in Cuba are measured from a diamond inset in the floor.

3 Malecón

Stretching west from Paseo de Martí, the Malecón – Havana's seafront boulevard **(above)** – is the perfect place for a sunset stroll.

4 Avenida de los Presidentes

Flanked by mansions, this broad boulevard slopes north to the Malecón and is studded with monuments to deceased heroes and heads of state.

5 Paseo de Martí

Sloping from Parque Central to the Malecón, this tree-shaded boulevard – known colloquially by its former name of Prado – is a great place to meet locals. The area is full of school kids at play during the day.

⑥ Plaza de la Revolución

A vast, austere square surrounded by government buildings such as the Ministry of the Interior (left), this is the heart of state affairs, best visited during the May Day Parade when it is packed with people.

⑦ Parque Central

This attractive park (below) makes a good starting point from which to explore the city. With a statue of national hero José Martí, it is surrounded by hotels and several city attractions. Baseball fans often gather here for lively debates.

BIOTECH SUCCESS

One of the world's most advanced biotechnology and genetic engineering industries is concentrated in the western Havana district of Siboney. The research facilities here are cutting edge in their field, and treatments for illnesses such as cancer, AIDS, and meningitis have been developed.

⑧ Hotel Nacional

A grandiose legacy of the 1930s, this landmark building is modeled on The Breakers, in Palm Beach, Florida. It boasts an international *Who's Who* list of past guests.

NEED TO KNOW

Universidad de La Habana: **MAP U2** ■ Calle L & San Lázaro ■ 7879 3488 ■ 9am–5pm Mon–Fri; closed Jul–Aug

Capitolio: **MAP V5** ■ Paseo de Martí & Calle Brasil ■ 7861 5519 ■ closed for renovation until 2017

Malecón: **MAP S1–W1**

Avenida de los Presidentes: **MAP T1–2**

Paseo de Martí: **MAP W1–2**

Plaza de la Revolución: **MAP T3**

Parque Central: **MAP V5**

Hotel Nacional: **MAP U1** ■ Calle O & Calle 21 ■ 7836 3564

Cementerio Colón: **MAP S3** ■ Avenida Zapata & Calle 12 ■ 7830 4517 ■ 8am–5pm daily. Adm: CUC$5

⑨ Cementerio Colón

Havana's huge cemetery features an astonishing collection of elaborate tombs. Many of Cuba's most famous personalities are buried here.

⑩ Miramar

This region of western Havana, developed in the 20th century, features avenues lined with mansions and plush hotels set amid age-old fig trees.

TOP 10 ★ Cordillera de Guaniguanico

The pine-clad mountains that begin a short distance west of Havana and run through northern Pinar del Río province are a nature lover's paradise of protected national parks sheltering endangered fauna. The mountains grow more rugged westward, where tobacco plants thrive, dramatic rock formations called *mogotes* tower over lush valleys, and huge cavern systems attract cavers. Centered on a village that itself is a National Historic Monument, the Valle de Viñales is rural Cuba at its most sublime.

Parque Nacional de Viñales **1**

This exquisite valley, the most scenic setting in Cuba, is remarkable for its limestone formations called *mogotes* **(right)**. Many of these massive structures are riddled with caves.

Soroa **2**

A lush retreat within the Sierra del Rosario Biosphere Reserve, Soroa **(above)** is famous for its hillside Orquideario – orchid garden – and scenic trails. Guests can enjoy treatments in a bath-house directly fed by the fresh mineral springs.

Las Terrazas **3**

Built as a model rural community, this mountain village is a center for ecotourism and is known for its artists' studios and trails that lead to beautiful water-falls and coffee farms.

Tobacco Farms **4**

The valleys of Pinar del Río are renowned as centers for the production of the nation's finest cigar tobacco, often seen drying in sheds. The fields are tilled by ox-drawn ploughs even today.

Gran Caverna de Santo Tomás **5**

Take a guided tour through Cuba's largest cave system – 28 miles (45 km) of galleries adorned with stalactites and stalagmites.

Rancho La Guabina **6**

This lakeside horse-breeding center is set amid hills with trails **(below)**. Horseback riding is offered, and the farm can be explored in horse carriages. It has a lovely boutique hotel.

9 Cueva del Indio

Deep inside a *mogote*, this huge cavern lit by artificial lighting has fabulous dripstone formations. Having walked the floodlit trail, visitors can ride through an underground river **(left)** on a motorized boat.

MOGOTES

These round-topped rock formations are the remains of a limestone plateau. Over millions of years, water dissolved the rock, creating caverns. When the ceilings collapsed, they left these free-standing pillars. Visit the Mural de la Prehistoria at Valle de Viñales, painted on a *mogote* by Leovigildo González Morillo.

10 Viñales

Harking back to a bygone era, this quintessentially colonial village exudes unspoiled charm. Ox-carts plod through quiet streets lined with traditional homes fronted by old-fashioned arcades.

7 Cueva de los Portales

Located at an amazing height of 100 ft (30 m), this cavern was Che Guevara's headquarters during the Cuban Missile Crisis. It has Che's old iron bed as well as giant stalagmites and stalactites.

8 Hiking

Las Terrazas, Soroa, and Viñales all have official trails. A licensed guide – required for hiking into the mountains – can be hired at each of these starting points.

NEED TO KNOW

Parque Nacional de Viñales: **MAP B2** ▪ (48) 79 6144

Soroa: **MAP C2** ▪ (48) 52 3871 ▪ Adm: CUC$3, with guide

Las Terrazas: **MAP C2** ▪ Autopista Habana-Pinar del Río, km 51 ▪ (48) 57 8700

Gran Caverna de San Tomás: **MAP B2** ▪ Parque Nacional de Viñales ▪ (48) 68 1214 ▪ 9:30am–3:30pm daily. Adm: CUC$10

Rancho La Guabina: **MAP B3** ▪ Carretera de Luís Lazo, km 9.5 ▪ (48) 75 7616 ▪ 8am–5pm daily

Cueva de los Portales: **MAP C2** ▪ Carretera San Andrés, km 14 ▪ (48) 63 6749 ▪ 8am–5pm daily. Adm: CUC$1

Cueva del Indio: **MAP B2** ▪ Carretera Puerto Esperanza, km 36 ▪ (48) 77 8053 ▪ 9am–5pm daily. Adm: CUC$5

TOP 10 ⭐ Zapata Peninsula

Protected within a huge biosphere reserve, the Zapata Peninsula is covered in swampland and forests teeming with wildlife. The coast is lined with sandy beaches and coral reef, attracting scuba divers. Much of the population here works as *carboneros*, eking out a living making charcoal. The area is known for the Bahía de Cochinos (Bay of Pigs), site of the invasion *(see p37)*.

Laguna del Tesoro ①
Accessed via a 3-mile (5-km) canal, "Treasure Lake" **(right)** is named for the gold that Taíno Indians supposedly hid in its waters when Spanish *conquistadores* arrived. Boat tours visit a recreated Taíno village on an island that also hosts a resort hotel.

② Birding
Eighteen of Cuba's 22 endemic bird species *(see pp52–3)* inhabit Zapata, including *tocororo* and *zunzuncito* **(above)**. Flamingos tiptoe elegantly around Las Salinas lagoon, while sandhill cranes throng the reed beds.

③ Fishing
The saltwater shallows off southern Zapata teem with bonefish, while tarpon and *manjuarí* (alligator gar) inhabit the estuaries and tributaries of the Hatiguanico river.

④ Parque Nacional Ciénaga de Zapata
This vast wetland ecosystem can be explored on guided tours and boat trips. The mangroves, grasslands, and lagoons teem with wildlife.

⑤ Crocodile Farm
Visitors can photograph crocodiles **(left)** from an observation point overlooking the Boca de Guamá, which is Cuba's largest crocodile farm.

6 Museo Girón
Housing military hardware, including tanks and a Cuban air force plane (above), this museum features items relating to the Bay of Pigs invasion and the three-day battle that followed.

7 Central Australia
Castro's headquarters during the Bay of Pigs invasion in 1961 was in the former administrative offices of the now-defunct Central Australia sugar mill. A steam train excursion operates from here into the countryside.

8 Caleta Buena
This splendid cove (above) with coral-filled turquoise waters is perfect for snorkeling and scuba diving. White sands top the coral shoreline.

9 Cenote de los Peces
With peacock-blue waters, this exquisite natural pool is 33 ft (10 m) deep, and has a side tunnel that descends 230 ft (70 m). Named for the fish that swim in it, this is a popular spot for cave-diving enthusiasts.

LA VICTORIA

Trained by the CIA, the anti-Castro exiles who landed at the Bay of Pigs on April 17, 1961 intended to link up with counter-revolutionaries in the rugged Sierra del Escambray. The site was ill chosen, as the landing craft grounded on reefs. The invasion was finally doomed when President John F. Kennedy refused to authorize the US naval and air support.

NEED TO KNOW

Laguna del Tesoro: **MAP F3** ▪ (45) 91 3224 ▪ Boats depart Boca 8:30am–4pm daily

Parque Nacional Ciénaga de Zapata: **MAP E3** ▪ (45) 98 7249 ▪ Adm: CUC$15 (including guide)

Crocodile farm: **MAP F3** ▪ (45) 91 5666 ▪ 7am–7pm daily. Adm: CUC$5

Caleta Buena: **MAP F3** ▪ (45) 91 5589 ▪ 10am–5pm daily. Adm: CUC$15

Cenote de los Peces: **MAP F3** ▪ 9am–5pm daily

Museo Girón: **MAP F3** ▪ (45) 98 4122 ▪ 9am–5pm daily. Adm: CUC$2; camera CUC$1; guide CUC$1

▪ The Colibrí restaurant at Boca de Guamá serves crocodile meat (its specialty), lobster, and excellent mojitos.

10 Scuba Diving
Unspoiled coral reefs and a wall plunging 1,000 ft (305 m) lie close to the shore. Inland, *cenotes* – fresh water pit-caves – are suitable for experienced divers only.

TOP 10 Trinidad

Founded in 1514 by Diego Velázquez, Trinidad was made a UNESCO World Heritage Site in 1988. During the 17th and 18th centuries, the city was a wealthy slave-trading center and hub of sugar production, and its wealthy landowners and merchants erected fine homes and mansions. The cobblestone streets lined with pastel-colored houses have barely changed since then; Trinidad feels like a town that time has passed by. Unlike most Cuban cities, Trinidad sits on a hill and is cooled by near-constant breezes.

1 Convento de San Francisco de Asís

This ancient convent hosts a museum that recounts the fight against counter-revolutionaries *(see p37)*. The landmark bell tower **(right)** can be climbed for a commanding view of the historic center.

2 Plaza Mayor
This atmospheric, palm-shaded square **(above)** at the heart of the old city is surrounded by a cathedral and important mansions that today house museums and art galleries.

3 Shopping
Good bargains can be found at the crafts markets lining the streets, where locals sell hand-stitched lace and papier-mâché models of 1950s US automobiles.

5 Nightlife
Trinidad is rightly celebrated for its after-dark ambience and, in particular, for traditional performances by Afro-Cuban troupes.

6 Museo Romántico
The Palacio Brunet, now a museum, is furnished in period style. The beautiful architectural details include a carved cedar ceiling and *medio-puntos* – half-moon stained-glass windows.

Playa Ancón 4
This is an immaculate beach **(right)** with turquoise waters on a peninsula 6 miles (10 km) from Trinidad. It is the setting for three tourist hotels.

7 Casa de la Trova

Traditional music is played at the "House of the Troubador" (left), on Plazuela de Segarte. This 1777 mansion is adorned with murals.

8 Vale de los Ingenios

This broad valley to the east of Trinidad is dotted with the atmospheric ruins of centuries-old sugar mills, including Hacienda Manaca Iznaga, which has a tower that can be climbed (see p103).

NEED TO KNOW

Convento de San Francisco de Asís: **MAP Y1** ■ Calle Echerri 59 ■ (41) 99 4121 ■ 9am–5pm daily. Adm: CUC$1; cameras CUC$1

Plaza Mayor: **MAP Z1**

Museo Romántico: **MAP Z1** ■ Calle Echerri & Calle Bolívar ■ (41) 99 4363 ■ 9am–5pm Mon–Fri & alternate Sun. Adm: CUC$2, cameras CUC$1

Casa de la Trova: **MAP Z1** ■ Calle Echerri 29 ■ (41) 99 6445 ■ 10am–1pm daily. Adm: CUC$1 after 8pm

Museo Histórico: **MAP Y2** ■ Calle Bolívar 423 ■ (41) 99 4460 ■ 9am–5pm Mon–Thu, Sat & alternate Sun. Adm: CUC$2; cameras CUC$1

■ Locals may scam you to stay at *casas particulares*. Don't trust any claims that your *casa* has closed.

9 La Boca

This rocky beach has spectacular views of the Escambray mountains (Sierra del Escambray). The sands are a great place to mingle with the locals.

10 Museo Histórico

Housed in the Palacio Cantero (above), the exhibits, including a fountain that once spouted *eau de cologne*, tell the town's story.

Following pages Street in central Havana

Jardines del Rey

Rising from the Atlantic along the north shore of Ciego de Ávila and Camagüey provinces, this 280-mile- (450-km-) long archipelago, known as the King's Gardens, contains hundreds of islands. Three of the major cays are linked to the mainland by *pedraplenes* (causeways), although only Cayo Coco and Cayo Guillermo have tourist facilities. These twin isles are popular with package vacationers. Flamingos wander the inshore lagoons, while other birds inhabit a nature preserve. Unfortunately, the causeway to Cayo Coco blocks ocean currents, much to the detriment of marine ecology.

1 Playa de los Flamencos

This lovely strip of white sand, stretching for 3 miles (5 km), is one of Cuba's most beautiful beaches. The crystal-clear turquoise waters are shallow enough for wading up to 650 ft (200 m) from the shore.

2 Flamingos

Graceful flamingos **(above)** flock to the Laguna de los Flamencos from April to November. Parador La Silla is the best place to spot them flying overhead at sunrise and dusk.

3 Cayo Coco

With miles of sandy beaches, Cayo Coco is a haven for marine birds and a popular destination for families, divers, and water sports enthusiasts.

4 Cayo Guillermo

Connected to Cayo Coco by a raised highway, this island **(left)** is lined with beautiful, gently shelving beaches. Mangroves grow in the channel that separates the two islands. Dunes reach 59 ft (18 m) at Playa Pilar.

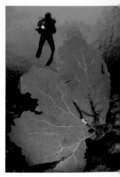

5 Water Sports

Resort hotels offer a wide range of beach and ocean activities, including banana-boat rides and catamarans. Crystal-clear visibility reveals an exciting underwater world **(above)** for snorkelers and divers.

6 Delfinario

Visitors can swim with trained dolphins at this open-water facility on Cayo Guillermo. Interactions also allow petting and hugging these intelligent mammals.

9 Cayo Sabinal

This virginal island's beaches are fringed by a coral reef. Wild pigs inhabit the scrub-covered isle, and flamingos grace the inshore lagoons.

10 Pedraplén

The highway linking Cayo Coco to the mainland runs ruler-straight across the Bahía de Perros, slicing it in two. At its north end, the road weaves through a series of small islands with herons, roseate spoonbills, and other wading birds.

7 Sol Meliá Beach Hotels

Spain's Sol Meliá has 28 hotels in Cuba, including six on Cayo Coco and Cayo Guillermo *(see p131)*, that offer a plethora of restaurants, water sports **(above)**, and creature comforts.

Horseback Riding 8

Exploring Cayo Coco and Cayo Guillermo on horseback is a fun excursion through the scrub and even along the beaches **(right)**.

🔟 ⭐ Camagüey

A cradle of Cuban culture, the "City of Tinajones" lies in the heart of cattle country and was laid out with irregular streets designed as a convoluted maze to thwart pirates. The historic center is full of well-preserved colonial plazas and cobbled streets featuring antique churches and convents, as well as colorful 17th- and 18th-century domestic buildings with red-tile roofs, lathe-turned wooden window grills, and spacious interior courtyards adorned with the city's trademark oversized jars called *tinajones*.

Plaza San Juan de Dios ③

A national monument, this plaza is lined with 18th-century pastel buildings **(right)** that reflect the local style. On the east side, a former church and military hospital houses a museum of colonial architecture.

Plaza del Carmen ①

Graced by a restored Baroque convent that functions as an art gallery, this cobblestone plaza is pedestrianized and features life-size ceramic figures of locals depicted in daily pursuits **(above)**.

④ Iglesia Sagrado Corazón de Jesús

This gracious, Neo-Gothic church dating from 1755 has been restored. It has a magnificent wooden ceiling, exquisite frescoes, and an elaborate gilt altar.

⑤ Iglesia Nuestra Señora de la Soledad

Built in 1776, this fine example of Cuban Baroque architecture has a lovely carved *alfarje* wood-paneled ceiling and painted pillars **(left)**. The revolutionary Ignacio Agramonte was baptized and married here.

⑥ Casa Natal Ignacio Agramonte

This former home of a local hero of Cuban Independence displays colonial furniture plus Agramonte's personal belongings, including his pistol. It has an intimate courtyard with *tinajones*.

② Catedral Nuestra Señora de la Merced

Dating from 1748, this Baroque church features noteworthy murals and the Santa Sepulcro, a figure of Christ atop a coffin cast from 23,000 silver coins.

7 Parque Agramonte

Dominated by a bronze equestrian statue of Ignacio Agramonte, the town's main square is surrounded by interesting colonial buildings, including the 18th-century cathedral with a six-story bell tower.

TINAJONES

Large earthenware jars up to 6 ft (2 m) wide called *tinajones* are a symbol of Camagüey. They were introduced by Catalonian immigrants in the early 1700s, and are used to collect rainwater, as well as for decorative purposes in courtyards and gardens.

NEED TO KNOW

MAP L3

Catedral Nuestra Señora de la Merced: Parque Agramonte

Iglesia Sagrado Corazón de Jesús: Parque Martí

Iglesia Nuestra Señora de la Soledad: Av. República & Agramonte

Casa Natal Ignacio Agramonte: Calle Agramonte 459 ▪ (32) 29 7116 ▪ 9am–4:45pm Tue–Sat, 9am–noon Sun. Adm CUC$2

Teatro Principal: Calle Padre Valencia ▪ (32) 29 3048

Museo Ignacio Agramonte: Av. de los Mártires ▪ (32) 28 2425 ▪ 9am–5pm Tue–Fri, 9am–4pm Sat, 9am–1pm Sun. Adm: CUC$2

▪ Beware of hustlers trying to guide you to a *casa particular (see p127)*.

8 Ballet de Camagüey

Second only to Havana's Ballet Nacional, Camagüey's renowned troupe **(below)** has toured over 40 countries. It was founded in 1967 by the prima ballerina Alicia Alonso *(see p43)*.

9 Teatro Principal

This Neo-Classical theater (1850) was rebuilt in 1926. Its marble staircase is lit by a gilt chandelier. It is the principal venue for the acclaimed Ballet de Camagüey.

10 Museo Ignacio Agramonte

This eclectic museum housed in the former Spanish cavalry headquarters focuses on local and natural history and displays a collection of art.

TOP 10 ⭐ Holguín

This sprawling industrial city, known as the "City of Squares," radiates around a compact colonial core arranged in an easily navigated grid. Its many historic plazas include Parque Calixto García, named for the general who liberated the city from the Spanish in 1872. With its abundance of small museums, Holguín has an especially active cultural life. Some tourists bypass the town to visit the hilltop tourist complex of Mirador de Mayabe or the beach resort of Guardalavaca, which offers various ecological and archaeological attractions as well as spectacular scuba diving.

2 Plaza Calixto García

The most prominent feature of this large, tree-shaded plaza is the marble monument of General Calixto García **(left)**. The busy square is also home to the city's main museums. Casa Natal de Calixto García, where the hero was born, is a block east of here.

5 Museo Provincial

The Neo-Classical building that houses this musem used to be a social club for the Spanish elite. Displays include historical artifacts, most notably the Hacha de Holguín – a pre-Columbian green peridot axe carved with human motifs.

3 Plaza San José

This cobbled square is the most intimate of the city's plazas and a pleasant place to sit on a bench beneath shady trees. Surrounded by colonial buildings, it is home to the Iglesia de San José, which is topped by a domed clocktower **(below)**.

1 Mirador de Mayabe

Offering a stunning vista over the Mayabe valley, this lookout is the setting for a fine hotel, a country-style restaurant, and a cliff-top pool with a bar where its famous beer-drinking donkey Pedro hangs out.

4 Plaza de la Marqueta

The ruins of a former market stand over this partially restored plaza, which features life-sized bronze figures. It is lined with shops including the Cuban Book Institute's Linotype print shop.

6 Casa de la Trova

This is one of Cuba's liveliest music venues with two programs daily. It is named for Faustino Oramas "El Guayabero" Osorio, who played the guitar here until his death in 2007, at the age of 96.

ORGANS

The Fábrica de Órganos at Carretera de Gibara 301 is the only Cuban factory still making mechanical hand-driven *órganos pneumáticos* (air-compression organs) using the traditional methods. They are fed with cards punched with the score. There is no guarantee that you will see or hear one being played.

NEED TO KNOW

Mirador de Mayabe: **MAP N4** ■ Alturas de Mayabe ■ (24) 42 2160 ■ 9am–7pm daily. Adm: CUC$2

Casa Natal de Calixto García: **MAP N4** ■ Frexes & Miró ■ (24) 42 5610 ■ 9am– 5pm Tue–Sat, 10am– 6pm Sun. Adm: CUC$1

Museo Provincial: **MAP N4** ■ Calle Frexes 198 ■ (24) 46 3395 ■ 8am–4:30pm Tue–Sat, 8am–noon Sun. Adm: CUC$1; cameras CUC$1

Playa Guardalavaca: **MAP P4**

Chorro de Maíta: **MAP N4** ■ Carretera Guardalavaca-Banes ■ (24) 43 0201 ■ 9am–5pm Mon–Sat (to 1pm Sun). Adm: CUC$2

■ Holguín bustles with events during Semana de la Cultura Holguinera.

⑦ Playa Guardalavaca

A one-hour drive northeast of Holguín, this resort is lined with wonderful beaches and unspoiled coral reefs **(above)** that tempt diving enthusiasts.

⑧ Gibara

A windswept coastal town, Gibara was once a prominent port protected by a fortress. Known as "Villa Blanca" (White City), it is packed with colonial buildings. It also has several museums, and is home to an annual festival of low-budget cinema.

⑨ Chorro de Maíta

This burial place, Cuba's largest pre-Columbian Indian site **(below)**, is an archaeological treasure with skeletons and funerary offerings on display. Adjacent to it is a re-created Indian village called Aldea Taína.

⑩ Loma de la Cruz

With views over the town, this hill is named for the Holy Cross at its summit and can be reached via 485 steps. It is the site for the Romerías de Mayo pilgrimage every May.

🔟⭐ Santiago de Cuba

The country's second-oldest and second-largest city has a flavor all its own as the most African, and the most musical city, in Cuba. It was founded in 1511 on the hilly east shore of a deep, flask-shaped bay. Its colonial core is full of historic buildings, while its fascinating past as the second capital of Cuba is enriched by its importance as a hotbed of political upheaval. Fidel Castro studied here and later initiated the Revolution with an attack on the Moncada barracks. Santiago explodes with colorful frenzy during Carnaval each July.

① El Morro

At the entrance to Santiago Bay, the 17th-century El Morro castle **(above)** offers stunning coastal vistas. Soldiers in period costume march onto the ramparts and fire a cannon at dusk.

③ Plaza de la Revolución

This vast plaza was used primarily for political rallies and features a massive monument of General Antonio Maceo.

④ Reserva de la Biosfera Baconao

Just east of Santiago, this reserve features a dolphinarium, a classic car museum, artist communities, on a mountain coffee estate, and a lovely tropical garden *(see p114)*.

② Museo Emilio Bacardí

Visitors can view colonial-era armaments, relics from the slave trade, and a superlative body of paintings and sculptures in Cuba's oldest museum **(above)**.

⑤ Parque Céspedes

At the heart of the city, this square is lined with historic buildings such as the Casa de Diego Velázquez, and the Catedral de la Asunción.

NEED TO KNOW

MAP P6

El Morro: Carretera al Morro, km 7.5 ▪ (22) 69 1569 ▪ 8:30am– 9:30pm daily. Adm: CUC$4; cameras CUC$5

Museo Emilio Bacardí: Calle Pío Rosado ▪ (22) 62 8402 ▪ 9am–5pm Mon– Sat, 9am–3pm Sun. Adm: CUC$2; cameras CUC$5

Cementerio Santa Ifigenia: Avenida Capitán Raúl Perozo ▪ (22) 63 2723 ▪ 8am–5pm daily. Adm: CUC$3; cameras CUC$5

Cuartel Moncada: Avenida Moncada ▪ (22) 66 1157 ▪ 9am–4:30pm Tue–Sat, 9am–12:30pm Sun & Mon. Adm: CUC$2; cameras CUC$5

6 Vista Alegre
A leafy residential district, Vedado features mansions and Modernist homes. The Casa del Caribe and Museo de las Religiones Populares honor the city's rich Afro-Cuban culture.

8 Cementerio Santa Ifigenia
Many important figures are buried here, including José Martí (see p37), whose guard of honor changes every half hour. Fidel Castro will also be interred here one day.

VIRGEN DE LA CARIDAD DEL COBRE

Miraculous powers are ascribed to the Virgin of Charity, Cuba's patron saint, who is represented as a black Virgin Mary holding a black Christ. According to Cuban legend, three fishermen were caught in a storm in 1608 and survived because a statue of the Virgin appeared, calming the seas for them.

Panoramic view of Santiago de Cuba

9 Cuartel Moncada
The setting for Castro's attack on July 26, 1953 (see p37), this former military barracks **(above)** is today a school housing the Museo Histórico 26 de Julio recalling the failed venture, as well as exhibits recounting a general history of Cuba.

7 El Cobre
This village is famous for the Basílica de Nuestra Señora de la Caridad del Cobre, Cuba's most important church, where pilgrims gather to pray to the Virgin of Charity.

10 Plaza Dolores
Popular, tree-shaded Plaza Dolores is a pleasant place to relax. The former Iglesia de Nuestra Señora de los Dolores church **(left)** on the east side now functions as a venue for classical concerts.

TOP10 ⭐ Baracoa

Tucked inside a broad bay enfolded by mountains, Baracoa sits at the far northeast corner of Cuba. It was founded in 1511 as the island's first settlement and capital. When governor Velázquez moved to Santiago, a long period of isolation set in. Locals claim that the Bahía de Miel was the site of Columbus' first landing in Cuba in 1492, and that the flat-topped mountain he described is El Yunque, which rises behind Baracoa. Lined with wooden houses in local style, the town now buzzes with tourists, and is particularly popular with independent travelers.

3 Plaza Independencia

This small plaza **(right)** has a bust of the heroic Indian leader Hatüey in front of the Catedral de Nuestra Señora de la Asunción, where you can see a wooden cross said to have been brought to Cuba by Columbus.

1 Fuerte Matachín

Guarding the eastern entrance to town, this tiny fortress contains a museum that traces the history of Baracoa and a collection of polymitas – colored snails **(above)** particular to the region.

2 Bahía de Baracoa

This flask-shaped bay **(below)** to the west of town is lined by a gray-sand beach, backed by thickly forested Alturas de Baracoa mountains.

4 Museo Arqueológico

Full of fascinating drip-stone formations, the Cueva de Paraíso hosts an archaeological mu-seum with Taíno Indian artifacts and a funerary cave displaying skeletons.

5 Hotel El Castillo

Built to repel the British, the Castillo de Seboruco fortress now houses a hotel (see p129) with sensational views.

6 Regional Cuisine

Baracoa is known for its cuisine based on creative uses of coconut, such as the *cucurucho*, a coconut dessert mixed with fruits and honey.

8 Punta Maisí
Accessed via a paved mountain road, this most easterly point of the island of Cuba is marked by a lighthouse, built in 1862. On a clear day, it is possible to see Haiti from here.

POLYMITAS

The polymita genus of snail, endemic to the Baracoa region, is remarkable for its multi-colored shell with a whorled pattern. Each snail has a unique pattern and color. With a dwindling population, the polymita is now endangered. You are advised not to buy any shells offered for sale.

NEED TO KNOW

MAP R5

Fuerte Matachín: Calle Martí ▪ (21) 64 2122 ▪ 8am–noon, 2–6pm Mon–Sat, 8am–noon Sun. Adm: CUC$1

Catedral de Nuestra Señora de la Asunción: Plaza Independencia ▪ (21) 64 3352 ▪ 8–11am, 4–7pm Mon–Fri, 8–11am, 5–9pm Sat, 8am–noon Sun

Museo Arqueológico: 8am–5pm daily. Adm: CUC$3; cameras CUC$1

▪ If you are curious to see the endangered rodent-like jutía and insect-eating almique, head to the Parque Zoológico, which lies 4 miles (6 km) east of the town.

▪ The colorful El Poeta is a great place to try local food, served in an unusual style *(see p117)*.

7 El Yunque
An anvil-shaped mountain formation **(above)**, El Yunque rises above lush rainforests that provide an ideal habitat for rare species of flora and fauna.

9 Hiking
Guided hikes into the rainforests to the south of town lead into the mountains. Birders still hope to spot the ivory-billed woodpecker, threatened by extinction.

10 Playa Duaba
This black-sand beach west of Baracoa features a monument to General Antonio Maceo, who landed here in 1895 and fought the first battle of the War of Independence.

The Top 10
of Everything

Valle de Viñales

Moments in History

1 c.500 BC: Taíno Culture
The Taíno people arrived from the Orinoco region of South America on the island they called Cuba. Worshipping gods of nature, this peaceful society was organized into villages led by *caciques* (chieftains).

2 1492: Columbus Arrives
The Genoese explorer sighted Cuba during his first voyage and renamed it Juana. In 1509, Columbus' son Diego conquered the island and exterminated the Taínos. *Conquistador* Diego Velázquez founded the first town, Baracoa, in 1511.

3 1762: The English Occupy Cuba
The golden age of the Spanish colony ended when English troops seized Havana. England opened Cuba to free trade and expanded the slave trade. In 1763, Havana was returned to Spain in exchange for Florida.

4 1868: Ten Years' War
Landowner Carlos Manuel de Céspedes freed his slaves and revolted against Spanish rule. A guerrilla war ensued, in which towns were razed and the economy devastated. Later, US companies bought up Cuban sugar plantations.

War of Independence (1895–98)

5 1895: War of Independence
Exiled nationalist José Martí returned to lead the fight for independence. Though martyred in battle, his forces gained the upper hand, but were sidelined after the USS *Maine* was destroyed in Havana harbor. The US declared war on Spain, and invaded Cuba, occupying it.

6 1902: Independence
Following four years of US military rule, Washington granted the island its independence. A period of mostly corrupt government followed, while US corporations came to dominate the Cuban sugar-based economy. In 1906, following a revolt against president Palma, the US re-occupied the island for four years.

Capture of Havana by the English in 1762

7 1953: Castro Attacks Moncada

Castro launched the Cuban Revolution with an audacious attack timed to coincide with carnival celebrations in Santiago. The assault failed, and 64 captured rebels were tortured to death. Fidel delivered a brilliant defense at his trial, during which he gained national sympathy.

Fidel Castro enters Havana

8 1959: Revolution Triumphs

On New Year's Eve 1958, General Fulgencio Batista fled Cuba, and Castro delivered a victory speech in Santiago in advance of his triumphant journey to Havana. A newly formed democratic government was quickly usurped by Castro, who allied with the Soviet Union and initiated dramatic reforms.

9 1961: Bay of Pigs Invasion

CIA-trained Cuban exiles stormed ashore to assist Cuban-based counter-revolutionaries in toppling Castro. The attack was repelled, and Castro took advantage of popular sentiment against the US-inspired invasion to announce that Cuba would be socialist.

10 1991: Período Especial Begins

Thirty years of economic support ended overnight when the Soviet Union collapsed. The economy imploded, and Cubans faced extreme hardship, triggering a mass exodus to the US on flimsy rafts. Since 1994, the crisis has eased with a tourism boom helping to promote recovery.

TOP 10 NATIONAL FIGURES

1 Christopher Columbus (1451–1506)
Visionary Genoese explorer and the first European to sight Cuba on October 28, 1492.

2 Hatüey (died 1512)
Heroic Taíno chieftain who led resistance to Spanish colonial rule and was burned at the stake.

3 Carlos Manuel de Céspedes (1819–74)
The "Father of the Homeland" freed his slaves and launched the wars for independence.

4 José Martí (1853–95)
Cuba's foremost national hero, a writer and leader martyred in battle.

5 Máximo Gómez (1836–1905)
Dominican-born general and supreme commander of the Cuban liberation army.

6 Antonio Maceo Grajales (1845–96)
Successful guerrilla leader in the independence wars, Grajales was killed in battle.

7 Calixto García (1839–98)
Second-in-command of the independence army, and liberator of many Spanish-held cities.

8 Gerardo Machado (1871–1939)
Corrupt dictator who ruled Cuba with an iron fist between 1924 and 1933, when he was forced into exile.

9 Fulgencio Batista (1901–73)
Mulatto general who seized power in 1934 and ruled Cuba until he fled on New Year's Eve in 1958.

10 Fidel Castro (b.1926)
Former head of state who led the Revolution. Castro held power for five decades.

Calixto Garcia

🔟 Revolutionary Sites

Salon de los Espejos (Hall of Mirrors) at the Museo de la Revolución

1 Museo de la Revolución

The struggle for independence, the effort to topple Batista, and the subsequent building of socialism are highlighted in this museum *(see p13)*. It is housed in the former presidential palace, which was built in 1920 and fitted with lavish interior decoration. The caricatures in the "Corner of Cretins" poke fun at Batista and at US presidents Reagan, and Bush Sr and Jr.

2 Presidio Modelo

This model prison, completed in 1936, accommodated Fidel and Raúl Castro as well as 25 other revolutionaries sentenced to imprisonment following the Moncada attack. The hospital wing where they slept is now a museum *(see p87)*, while Fidel's private room with its marble bathroom contains a collection of the books he read during his years of incarceration.

3 Granma Memorial

MAP V4 ■ Calle Colón, Havana ■ 7862 4091 ■ Open 9am–5pm daily ■ Adm

The *Granma*, the vessel in which Castro sailed to Cuba with his guerrilla army, is displayed within a glass case in an open-air plaza to the rear of the Museo de la Revolución. Exhibits at the memorial include military hardware left over from the Bay of Pigs invasion.

4 Mausoleo y Museo del Segundo Frente

MAP P5 ■ Avenida Frank País, Mayarí Arriba ■ (22) 42 5749 ■ Open 9am–4:30pm Mon–Sat, 9am–noon Sun

The small town of Mayarí Arriba commemorates combatants of the Second Front, led by Raúl Castro. The complex includes a museum exhibiting armaments and warplanes, and a landscaped mausoleum, framed by royal palms, includes the future grave of Raúl.

Presidio Modelo

5 La Comandancia de la Plata

MAP M6 ■ Parque Nacional Pico Turquino, 5 miles (8 km) from Villa Santo Domingo ■ EcoTur, Bayamo; (23) 48 7006; departures from 9am ■ Adm

A permit and guide are required to visit Castro's former guerrilla headquarters. Visits can be booked at the Ecotur office in Hotel Sierra Maestra.

6 Cuartel Moncada

Bullet holes riddle the walls of this former military barracks that sustained attacks by Castro's rebels on July 26, 1953, in the opening salvo to topple Batista. The building is now a school and includes the Museo Histórico 26 de Julio (see p31), full of gory mementos.

7 Monumento del Che

A massive bronze figure of Che Guevara stands over bas-reliefs of Che in combat. Beneath and to the rear, the Museo del Che is Cuba's principal museum dedicated to the Argentinian revolutionary, whose remains are interred in an adjacent mausoleum (see p97).

8 Complejo Histórico Abel Santamaría

MAP P6 ■ Av. de los Libertadores, Santiago de Cuba ■ (22) 62 4119 ■ Open 9am–5pm Mon–Thu & Sun, 1–5pm Fri ■ Adm

A Modernist bas-relief of revolutionary Abel Santamaría overlooks

Complejo Histórico Abel Santamaría

this park, where his rebel corps fired on Moncada. A museum honoring Santamaría is housed in the colonial former Civil Hospital Saturnino Lora building, later used for the trial of Fidel Castro.

Monumento del Che

9 Museo de la Lucha Clandestina

MAP P6 ■ Calle Rabí 1, Santiago de Cuba ■ (22) 62 4689 ■ Open 9am–4:45pm Tue–Sun ■ Adm

This museum in the former headquarters of Batista's police force tells the story of the brave M-26-7 revolutionaries in Santiago who assaulted the building in November 1956.

10 Granjita Siboney

MAP P6 ■ Carretera a Siboney, km 13.5 ■ (22) 39 9168 ■ Open 9am–1pm Mon, 9am–5pm Tue–Sun ■ Adm

Castro launched the attack on Moncada from this farmhouse (see p40), which is now a museum. Batista's forces then attacked it and dumped the rebel bodies here.

Moments in Fidel Castro's Life

1 Birth and Childhood

Born on August 13, 1926, to a rural patriarch and his maid at Birán in Holguín province, Fidel Castro was raised by his mother and was not formally recognized by his father until he turned 17.

Fidel Castro as a child

2 Jesuit Schooling

Castro was educated by Jesuits in Santiago de Cuba, and later at Belén College in Havana. Although combative, he excelled in his studies and was named Cuba's top student athlete.

3 University

Castro entered the University of Havana law school in 1945, where he became embroiled in politics as a student leader, and graduated in 1950. He made national headlines several times as an outspoken critic of the government.

4 Attack on Moncada

After Batista overthrew the constitutional government and cancelled elections in March 1953, Castro initiated a legal petition against him. It failed, and he launched his revolution with an assault on the Moncada Barracks on July 26, 1953.

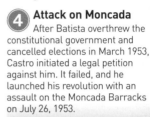

Moncada Barracks, with bullet holes

5 Prison

After giving his impassioned "History Will Absolve Me" speech in 1953, Castro was sent to prison for 15 years. He used the time to organize his forces. Amnestied in May 1955, he set up a guerrilla army during exile in Mexico.

6 War in the Sierra Maestra

After his exile ended, Castro initiated a plan to return to Cuba. On landing in the Granma province, his forces were ambushed, but Castro, Raúl Castro, and Che Guevara escaped and established their headquarters (see p39). Castro directed the opposition from here, winning several battles and slowly taking control of Cuba.

Castro giving rifle training to new recruits in his revolutionary army

7 Batista Toppled

Castro pledged to support a provisional democratic government after his forces ousted Batista in 1959. Meanwhile, separate guerrilla columns, led by Che Guevara and Camilo Cienfuegos, won key victories. When Santa Clara fell to Che Guevara's troops on New Year's Eve, 1958, Batista fled the country, and Castro triumphantly returned to Havana.

8 Bay of Pigs

A democratic government was founded, but Castro usurped it and initiated dramatic socialist reforms. This resulted in a massive exodus of Cubans. A group of unhappy exiles, trained by the CIA, landed at the Bay of Pigs on April 17, 1961 to invade Cuba, but were quickly defeated.

9 Cuban Missile Crisis

In December 1961, Castro declared Cuba a Marxist-Leninist state. He signed a pact with the Soviet Union, which installed nuclear missiles in Cuba in 1962. However, the US President Kennedy demanded their withdrawal. The nations stood on the brink of nuclear war until Soviet President Khrushchev backed down.

Soviet freighter Anosov, thought to have been carrying missiles to Cuba

10 Castro Resigns

Castro announced on July 31, 2006 that he had an acute intestinal illness. Handing temporary power to his brother, Raúl Castro, he underwent surgery and began a long recovery. Fidel resigned on February 19, 2008; Raúl was elected president on February 24, 2008.

TOP 10 REVOLUTIONARY HEROES

Che Guevara

1 Raúl Castro (1931–)
The younger brother of Fidel, a lifelong communist and the current Cuban president.

2 Camilo Cienfuegos (1932–59)
Chief of Staff in Fidel's guerrilla army. He went missing on a night flight in October 1959, and neither his plane nor he have ever been found.

3 José Antonio Echeverría (1932–57)
Student leader who gave a dramatic "Three Minutes of Truth" speech on Cuban national radio before being shot dead by a police patrol.

4 Che Guevara (1928–67)
Doctor-turned-revolutionary who became Minister of Finance & Industry and steered Cuba into socialism.

5 Julio Antonio Mella (1903–29)
The founder of the Cuban Communist Party, he was murdered in Mexico.

6 Jesús Menéndez (1911–48)
Socialist labor agitator who worked on behalf of local sugarcane workers.

7 Frank País (1934–57)
A principal leader in the M-26-7 movement, País was murdered by Batista's police.

8 Abel Santamaría (1927–53)
Castro's probable successor, Santamaría was killed after the Moncada attack.

9 Haydée Santamaría (1923–80)
Abel's sister was captured at Moncada, but managed to survive the torture.

10 Celia Sánchez (1920–80)
Middle-class socialist who ran the supply line for Castro's guerrilla army and later became his secretary.

Writers and Artists

Cuban writer Alejo Carpentier

Alejo Carpentier (1904–80)

Carpentier is known for his cultural journalism focused on Afro-Cuban traditions. He was sent into exile for opposing General Machado. After the Revolution (see p37), he headed Cuba's state publishing house.

② Amelia Peláez (1896–1968)

Influenced by Matisse and Picasso, this ceramicist and painter is best known for her vast mural of blue, black, and white glass tiles adorning Hotel Habana Libre (see p77).

③ José Martí (1853–95)

Perhaps the leading Latin American essayist, poet, and journalist of the 19th century, Martí led the Independence movement (see p36). He wrote profusely for the cause of social justice, pan-Americanism, and liberty.

④ Wifredo Lam (1902–82)

Born in Sagua la Grande, Lam befriended many leading European painters while living in Paris. His works reflect Afro-Cuban culture.

⑤ Dulce María Loynaz (1902–97)

The doyenne of Cuban poetry, Loynaz went into relative seclusion following the Revolution, after her husband fled Cuba. Her works were rediscovered in the 1980s, when she re-engaged with literary circles. An erotic intensity infuses many of her works.

⑥ Nicolás Guillén (1902–89)

Considered the poet laureate of Cuba, Guillén's African heritage is reflected in his distinctive *poesía negra* (black poetry). He joined the Communist Party at an early age and became president of the National Union of Writers and Artists.

⑦ René Portocarrero (1912–85)

One of Cuba's masters, Portocarrero is well represented in the Museo

The Jose Martí Monument in Parque Central Havana

Diablito (1966), by internationally renowned artist René Portocarrero

Nacional de Bellas Artes *(see p12)*, his murals are also in the Teatro Nacional and Hotel Habana Libre. His work is infused with religious icons.

Guillermo Cabrera Infante (1929–2005)

This critic, journalist, and novelist is best known for *Tres Tristes Tigres*, his seminal novel about the sordid era of pre-revolutionary Havana. Post-Revolution, he edited a key literary magazine before being exiled for criticizing Castro's government.

⑨ José Lezama Lima (1910–76)

A gay libertine known as much for his flamboyant lifestyle as for his Baroque writing, Lima was persecuted following the Revolution. Today he ranks among the Cuban literary elite. His most famous work is the semi-biographical *Paradiso*.

⑩ Manuel Mendive (b.1944)

Mendive is considered to be Cuba's most visionary and influential living artist. His works are both naive and highly erotic. A practising *santero* *(see pp48–9)*, Mendive is represented in museums around the world.

TOP 10 OTHER FAMOUS CUBANS

1 Carlos Finlay (1833–1915)
The doctor who discovered that yellow fever is transmitted by mosquitoes.

2 Gerardo Machado (1871–1939)
Corrupt and ruthless military leader who seized power in 1925 and fled in 1933 *(see p37)*.

3 Fulgencio Batista (1901–73)
A sergeant who carried out a military coup and ran Cuba as a brutally repressive dictator *(see p37)*.

4 José Raúl Capablanca (1888–1942)
The "Mozart of chess," as he was known, held the World Chess Championship title from 1921 to 1927.

5 Alberto Díaz Gutiérrez (1928–2001)
This photographer, better known as Alberto Korda, shot the iconic image of Che Guevara.

6 Tomás Gutiérrez Alea (1928–96)
A brilliant film-maker, "Titón" was at the forefront of New Latin American cinema in the 1960s and 70s.

7 Eligio Sardiñas (1910–88)
Christened "Kid Chocolate" by his fans, this boxing prodigy was also a wild party man.

8 Alicia Alonso (b.1920)
Cuba's *prima ballerina assoluta* who founded the National Ballet of Cuba.

9 Teófilo Stevenson (1952–2012)
Considered one of the greatest boxers of all time, this Olympic gold medal winner refused to turn professional.

10 Ana Fidelia Quirot (b.1963)
A track and field athlete who survived severe burns to win a silver medal at the 1996 Olympics.

Alicia Alonso and Igor Youskevitch

American Legacies

Classic American cars on a Cuban street

1 American Autos

Time seems to have stood still for five decades on Cuban roads, where one in every five cars dates back to before the Revolution *(see p37)*. Most are American classics from the 1950s – including many iconic models that vanished from US roads years ago.

2 Art Deco

Cuban cities are graced with Art Deco buildings that date back to the 1930s and the heyday of Hollywood movies. The finest are the cinemas, often with rounded architectural elements and horizontal banding. These designs exemplify the architects' desire to imbue local buildings with slick, streamlined forms, reflecting the great age of transport.

3 Harley-Davidsons

Many pre-revolutionary Harleys still roar around the streets of Cuba, maintained by passionate *harlistas* who are dedicated to keeping their "hogs" on the road by whatever means.

Industriales baseball team

4 Baseball

Americans introduced baseball to Cuba in the mid-19th century. Today, the island produces some excellent players. Cuban teams regularly defeat US teams at the Olympic Games.

5 US Naval Base
MAP Q6

When the US government wrote Cuba's Constitution in 1902 *(see p36)*, it included a clause called the Platt Amendment, which granted itself a perpetual lease on Guantánamo Bay. Despite thawing relations between the US and Cuba, the naval base remains a bone of contention. The US government writes a check every year for the annual lease, but the Castros *(see pp40–41)* refuse to cash it.

Art Deco Bacardi Building, Havana

Hotel Nacional

Symbolic of Havana's decadent pre-revolutionary heyday, this hotel was built in 1930 in Spanish Neo-Classical style and was closely associated with the Mafia. Actor Marlon Brando and supermodel Naomi Campbell feature in the hotel's celebrity guest list *(see p15)*.

7 Malecón

Havana's seafront boulevard was laid out in 1902 by US Army General Leonard Woods. Now officially known as Avenida Antonio Maceo, it is lined with late 19th-century buildings and high-rise hotels *(see p14)*.

8 Hotel Habana Libre

This national monument opened in March 1958 as the Havana Hilton. Built in Modernist style with 630 rooms, it was the largest and tallest hotel in Latin America. The hotel also once served as Fidel Castro's headquarters *(see p77)*.

9 Ernest Hemingway

The famous US author first came to Cuba in 1932 to fish for marlin. He fell in love with the island, and it was here that he wrote *For Whom the Bell Tolls*. In 1940 he bought Finca Vigía *(see p47)* outside Havana, his home for 20 years.

10 Steam Trains

Creaking engines and carriages piled with sugarcane are a common sight in Cuba, which has about 50 working steam trains – more than any other country except China. Most were made in Philadelphia in the 1920s.

 Cuban steam train

TOP 10 AMERICAN AUTOS

1955 Chevrolet Bel-Air

1 1955 Chevrolet Bel-Air
This was a perfectly proportioned 1950s icon.

2 1958 Edsel Corsair
Launched in 1958, the Edsel Corsair's styling drew more laughs than praise. Production of the flamboyant folly ended the following year.

3 1959 Cadillac Eldorado
Reflecting the pinnacle of exorbitant late-1950s styling, this rocket-like car was inspired by the space race.

4 1951 Chevrolet Styline
This Chevy was the most commonly seen classic car in Cuba.

5 1950 Studebaker Champion
Its unmistakable bullet-nose design proved to be popular with Cubans.

6 1951 Kaiser Traveler
Ahead of its time, this excellent car had many safety features that the US government would later mandate.

7 1951 Pontiac Chieftain
This car had a likeness of a Native American chieftain on its hood, which lit up when the headlights were on.

8 1953 Buick Super
Famed for its "grinning tooth" grill, this car had a Dynaflow three-speed transmission nicknamed "Dynaslush" on account of its slow responsiveness.

9 1951 Hudson Hornet
Its ground-hugging profile and power made it a winner in stock-car racing.

10 1952 Oldsmobile Super 88
This behemoth had power steering and a lightweight body that promised effortless "one finger" parking.

🔟 Museums

Museo Nacional de Bellas Artes

1 Museo Nacional de Bellas Artes

This fine arts museum boasts Ancient Egyptian, Greek, and Roman art, and the works of European Old Masters. The Cuban section demonstrates the vitality and range of homegrown art, from the colonial period to the contemporary era *(see p12)*.

2 Museo de Artes Decorativas

MAP T1–T2 ▪ Calle 17 502, Vedado, Havana ▪ 7832 0924 ▪ Open 9am–5pm Tue–Sat ▪ Adm

Lavish furnishings fill this former Beaux Arts residence of a Cuban countess and reveal the tastes of the 19th-century ruling classes – from the French Rococo furniture and 17th-century Italian sculptures to the pink marble Art Deco bathroom.

3 Museo de la Ciudad

MAP X4 ▪ Calle Tacón, Plaza de Armas, Havana ▪ 7866 8183 ▪ Open 9:30am–5pm Tue–Sun ▪ Adm

The museum in the Palacio de los Capitanes Generales covers the history of Havana. Exhibits include the city's first cemetery and a throne room built for the king of Spain, who never actually visited.

Museo de la Ciudad

4 Museo de Arquitectura Colonial

MAP H4 ▪ Plaza Mayor, Trinidad ▪ (41) 99 3208 ▪ Open 9am–5pm Mon–Sat ▪ Adm

The former mansion of the Sánchez-Iznaga family is today dedicated to colonial architecture, with excellent displays that trace the evolution of Trinidad's unique style, from the town's founding to the 20th century.

5 Museo Napoleónico

MAP U2 ▪ Calle San Miguel 1159, Vedado, Havana ▪ 7879 1460 ▪ Open 9:30am–5pm Tue–Sat (to noon Sun) ▪ Adm

This museum, in a 1920s palazzo, is replete with paintings, sculptures, and mementos of Napoleon Bonaparte.

Museo Napoleónico

6 Museo Oscar María de Rojas

MAP F2 ▪ Calzada between Vives and Jénez, Cárdenas ▪ (45) 52 2417 ▪ Open 9am–5pm Tue–Sat, 9am–1pm Sun ▪ Adm

Each of this museum's 14 salons has its own theme, from pre-Columbian culture to the Wars of Independence. Numismatists will enjoy the coin room. The Baroque 19th-century hearse is fascinating, as is the beautifully restored former governor's mansion that houses the museum.

7 Museo del Ron Havana Club

MAP X5 ▪ Fundación Destilería Havana Club, Avenida del Puerto 262, La Habana Vieja, Havana ▪ 7861 8051 ▪ Open 9am–5:30pm Mon–Thu, 9am–4:30pm Fri–Sun

This museum explores the history, brewing and distillation of Cuba's famous rum. Exhibits include a large-scale model of a sugar mill.

8 Museo Ernest Hemingway

Finca Vigía, Ernest Hemingway's former home, where he lived for 20 years, has been left untouched since his departure from Cuba in 1960. It still contains his books and hunting trophies. His sport-fishing vessel, *Pilar*, sits beneath a pavilion in the garden (see p76).

Museo Ernest Hemingway

9 Museo Emilio Bacardí

Cuba's oldest museum is housed in a Neo-Classical mansion. It boasts relics dating from the pre-Columbian era to the colonial period, as well as a fine collection related to slavery. Important Cuban art is found upstairs and includes works by Wifredo Lam (see p30).

10 Museo de la Guerra Hispano-Cubano-Norteamericano

MAP P6 ▪ Carretera a Siboney, km 13.5 ▪ (22) 39 9119 ▪ Open 9am–5pm Mon–Sat ▪ Adm

Situated outside the coastal hamlet of Siboney, this museum recalls the 1898 Spanish-American War, with many battle sites located nearby. Exhibits include artillery, torpedoes, uniforms, photographs, and bas-relief maps.

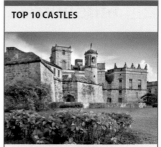

Santería

① Orishas

The many deities of *Santería* (an Afro-Caribbean religion) act as intermediaries between human beings and the supreme god, Olorún. Most *orishas* are avatars of Catholic saints, and each has his or her own costume, colors, symbols, and favorite foods, as well as specific abilities. Each believer has a personal *orisha*, who is considered to have the power over that person's destiny and is worshipped in daily life.

② Santeros

Santeros are practitioners, initiated formally into *Santería,* and are believed to be possessed by their personal *orisha* who guides them to a better life. *Santeros* are easily identified by their metal bracelets and colorful necklaces, which represent their particular *orisha*.

③ Altars

Altars are decorated with the attributes of the *orisha*, including their image in the form of a doll, devotional objects, and *ebó* (offerings). Tiny bells, maracas, and *agogó* (rattles) are played to awaken the *orisha*.

Ceramic and wood *Santería* symbols

Sacred *elekes*

④ Elekes

These necklaces of colored beads relate to specific *orishas*. While the uninitiated wear generic *elekes*, the bead patterns are determined by *santeros*, who prepare these necklaces using divination to find an order that reflects the *iyawó's* (initiate's) path.

⑤ Obi

Santería adherents believe that the wisdom of the *orishas* can be divined by dropping four pieces of coconut shell and studying the pattern they form. *Mojubas* (prayers) are said to invite the *orisha* to speak. These *obi* (oracles) are considered to help the believer reach wise decisions. At times, sacred palm seeds or cowrie shells are cast to invoke other oracles.

⑥ Initiation Ceremonies

Believers who seek a new path in life make a pact of veneration and obedience with their *orisha* through a week-long series of rituals. These require rigid adherence to meet the *orisha's* approval. The final initiation usually involves animal sacrifice. For a year thereafter, the *iyawó* will adhere to strict prescriptions of behavior and dress solely in white.

⑦ Ebó

Santería rites, known as *ebó*, require offerings of food and drink to the *orishas*. An *ebó* often involves ritual cleansing, and may include sacrificing chickens, pigeons, or goats. *Ebó* is also used to woo an *orisha*'s favor, or protect practitioners against witchcraft.

8 Wemilere
These ritual ceremonies are held to honor *orishas*. They comprise prayers, songs, and *batá* drumming. A believer may sometimes go into a trance – he or she is then believed to be possessed by the *orisha*.

9 Babalawos
Babalawos are the powerful high priests of *Santería*, and act as intermediaries to interpret the commands of the *orishas*. They use seashells, coconut husks, and seeds to divine the future and interpret the oracles. A *santero* might be required to train for a decade to reach the status of *babalawo*.

Babalawo interpreting the oracles

10 Batá
Of Yoruba origin, the sacred, hourglass-shaped *batá* drums – *itotele, iya,* and *okonkolo* – are carved of solid wood. Each has a different size and pitch. The drums are used during most important ceremonies and have their own rituals pertaining to their use and care.

Playing *batá* drums

Yemayá, the Virgin of Regla

1 Olorún
The principal god, often considered the androgynous sum of all divinity. He is the source of all spiritual energy.

2 Obatalá
The father of humankind represents wisdom and purity. He is androgynous and celebrates Our Lady of Mercy.

3 Ochún
The youngest *orisha*, Ochún is the sensual deity of water as well as the goddess of love.

4 Yemayá
The mother goddess is the giver of life and the protector of children and pregnant women.

5 Changó
The hot-tempered hero-god of thunder and lightning represents virility. His symbol is a double-bladed axe.

6 Babalu Aye
Associated with disease, Babalu Aye wears rags, walks with a crutch, and is accompanied by his dog.

7 Eleggua
God of the crossroads, Eleggua opens or closes the way of life. Cuban drivers often place Eleggua's *elekes* in their cars for protection.

8 Oggun
God of metal and war, he fights battles on behalf of petitioners and is often depicted with a machete.

9 Osain
This celibate deity represents the forces of nature. All initiations require his presence.

10 Oyá
She controls the fate of the injured and is aligned with St Barbara.

TOP 10 ORISHAS

🔟 Nature Trails

① Valle de Viñales
MAP B2

Surrounded by *mogotes*, Valle de Viñales has the most dramatic scenery in Cuba. Local tour agencies offer specialist hiking excursions along mountain trails, including climbs to the summit of *mogotes*; an official guide is obligatory.

Valle de Viñales

② El Yunque
The unique flat-topped El Yunque mountain *(see p33)* can be accessed by trail from Baracoa for a climb accompanied by a compulsory guide. The rewards are the staggering panoramic view and a chance to spot exotic birds.

③ Península de Guanahacabibes
MAP A3 ■ Centro de Visitantes: La Bajada, Sandino ■ (48) 75 0366 ■ Adm

At the far western tip of Cuba, this slender peninsula is covered with a rare expanse of tropical dry forest – a protected habitat for *jutías*, *jabalís*, and over 170 bird species. For birding and visits to caves, there are the Cueva de las Perlas and Sendero del Bosque al Mar trails.

④ Finca La Belén
MAP L4 ■ 27 miles (43 km) SE of Camagüey ■ (52) 19 5744 ■ Adm: for horseback and guided bird tours

A walk or horseback ride from this working farm, home to zebra and various exotic cattle, leads through semi-deciduous woodland and montane forests that help protect the different types of endemic plants including a rare cactus species. Bird-watchers will have a field day spotting parrots, hummingbirds, and other colorful birds.

⑤ Las Terrazas
This mountain resort *(see p16)* is Cuba's premier ecotourism destination, with trails, waterfalls, springs, and coffee plantations surrounded by forest. Hotel La Moka *(see p130)* provides decent lodgings.

Mineral Springs at Las Terrazas

Rock formations at Gran Parque Natural Topes de Collantes

6 Topes de Collantes

This resort complex on the southeast flank of the Sierra del Escambray (see p95) makes a perfect base for exploring the steep trails through scented pine forests and the El Nicho waterfall, which crashes into crystal-clear pools. The Parque Codina trail leads to an ancient coffee estate. Squawking parrots tear through the treetops, and the *tocororo* – Cuba's national bird (see p52) – can also often be spotted.

7 Parque Nacional Desembarco del Granma

This dry, dusty park is the starting point for several recommended trails that take visitors through a cactus-studded tropical forest. Bird-watching is a big draw here, and manatees are sometimes seen in mangrove lagoons. The El Guafe trail leads to a large cave full of limestone formations (see p115).

8 Pinares de Mayarí

MAP P5 ■ 12 miles (19 km) S of Mayarí, Holguín province ■ (24) 50 3308 ■ comercial@vpinares.co.cu

Take an excursion through a steep graded road to the wild pine-clad uplands of Pinares de Mayarí. This large area of montane wilderness is a popular base for guided hikes, such as the one to the Salto el Guayabo waterfall (see p116). A mountain resort that was created for the reigning Communist Party elite is now open to tourists.

9 Parque Nacional Alejandro Humboldt

Protecting the richest flora and fauna in Cuba, most of this wilderness is covered with dense rainforest and mangroves along the shore. Trails range from easy walks to challenging climbs to the Balcón de Iberia waterfall (see p116).

Orchid at Parque Nacional Alejandro Humboldt

10 Pico Turquino

MAP N6 ■ Departure 8am ■ Adm: permit including guides ■ Book visit at the Ecotur office, Hotel Sierra Maestra: Carretera Central, km 1.5, Bayamo; (23) 42 7972, (23) 42 7974

Cuba's highest mountain can be ascended from either north or south sides, the most popular starting point being Santo Domingo. At least two days are required, and guides are compulsory for the arduous climb. You will need to pre-arrange a second set of guides if you plan to traverse the mountain.

🔟 Animals and Birds

Cuban amazon parrot

4 Solenodon
You are unlikely to see one of these long-nosed, ant-eating mammals in the wild, as they are shy and nocturnal. Resembling a giant shrew, the solenodon is an endangered species, as it is easy prey for dogs and mongooses.

5 Tocororo
This pigeon-sized, forest-dwelling bird is a member of the trogon family. The *tocororo* is Cuba's national bird because its blue, white, and red plumage corresponds to the colors of the nation's flag. It has a serrated bill, concave-tipped tail, and is common throughout the island.

1 Cuban Amazon Parrot
The *cotorra*, or Cuban amazon parrot, an inhabitant of dry forests, was once found throughout Cuba. Now threatened, it is most easily seen in the Zapata swamps, on Isla de la Juventud, and in Parque Nacional Alejandro Humboldt. It performs noisy mating displays during the onset of the wet season.

2 Cuban Crocodile
Up to 16 ft (5 m) in length, the Cuban crocodile is endemic to the island and is far more aggressive than its cousin, the American crocodile, which is also found here. Despite being hunted to near extinction, the population has recovered thanks to a breeding program introduced by Fidel Castro.

3 Iguana
Resembling a small dragon, this leathery reptile inhabits offshore cays and feasts on leaves, fruit, and, occasionally, insects. It basks in the sun to become active, but seeks refuge from the mid-afternoon heat in cool burrows.

6 Flamingo
With legs that resemble carnation stalks this pink bird is the most attractive of Cuba's many estuary birds. Large flocks of flamingos inhabit the saltwater lagoons of Zapata. They primarily eat insect larvae, which contain a substance that gives them their bright color.

7 Polymita
These snails are remarkable for their colorful shells, whorled in patterns that are unique to each individual. The shells of these

Iguana

Polymita

multicolored mollusks can range from simple black-and-white spirals to blazing stripes of orange, yellow, and maroon. Unfortunately, Cuba's polymita population has been undergoing a decline.

8 Zunzuncito

The tiny Cuban hummingbird is so small, it is often mistaken for a bee; earning it the nickname "bee hummer." In fact, at only one inch (2.5 cm) long, it is the world's smallest bird. Nonetheless, this feisty bird defends its territory aggressively and has even been seen attacking vultures.

A *jutía*, or tree rat

9 Jutía

A shy arboreal rat, the endemic *jutía* looks like an overgrown guinea pig. This rabbit-sized herbivore is endangered by deforestation, illegal hunting, and predators. It inhabits many of the wilderness regions of Cuba, but is most likely to be seen in captivity. Many Cubans breed *jutías* for food.

10 Jabalí

The Cuban wild boar is known for its highly aggressive nature when threatened. Covered in thick bristles, it is common to lowland wilderness areas. The *jabalí* is hunted for sport – its meat is a local delicacy.

TOP 10 CUBAN TREES AND FLOWERS

1 Royal Palm
Cuba's silver-sheathed national tree is a beautiful palm with feather-like fronds.

2 Mangrove
Five species of mangroves grow along Cuba's shores, rising from the waters on a tangle of interlocking stilts.

3 Ceiba
This tree, with a huge limbless trunk topped by wide-spreading boughs, is attributed with magical-religious powers by believers of *Santería*.

4 Jagüey
Seeding atop host trees, this species drops roots to the ground and envelopes and chokes its host.

5 Sea Grape
This hardy shrub grows along shores and features broad, circular leaves and bunches of grape-like fruit.

6 Orchid
Hundreds of orchid species grow in Cuba from the plains to the mountains.

7 Creolean Pine
Native to the Caribbean, this species is found above about 5,000 ft (1,524 m).

8 Bougainvillea
Brightening many towns, the spectacular pink, purple, and bright red "flowers" of this shrub are, in fact, leaves surrounding tiny petals.

9 Flamboyán
Flowering flame-red, this wide-spreading tree emblazons the country in spring and summer.

10 Cork Palm
The endangered cork palm grows only in remote areas of the Cordillera de Guaniguanico (see p87).

Mangroves

🔟 Beach Resorts

1 Playas del Este
MAP H4

Meandering for several miles east of Havana, this sweeping stretch of beaches is popular with the capital's citizens as a weekend hangout. Pounding surf and a powerful undertow can be a deterrent to swimmers. The prettiest sections are Playa Santa María and Playa El Mégano, with gorgeous white sands and some beach facilities.

The pure white sands of Cayo Levisa

2 Cayo Levisa
MAP C2

This small island, ringed by white sands, an offshore coral reef, and mangroves, is renowned for its scuba diving. Coconut trees sway enticingly over a resort that has deluxe beachfront cabins along gorgeous white sands and turquoise waters.

3 Playa Sirena, Cayo Largo
MAP E4

Only a few miles from the all-inclusive hotels of Cayo Largo (see p86) this is a broad swathe of pure white sand with thatched restaurants. The waters are an alluring blue and perfect for water sports. Many Canadian and European tourists come to bask on the sands of this resort island. The water does get deep quickly, so children should be supervised at all times.

4 Playa Mayor, Varadero
MAP F1

Lined with hotels and beach-hut restaurants for almost its entire 7-mile (11.5-km) length, this long stretch of silvery sand is the most well-developed beach in Cuba. Still, there is enough space for everyone, and the peacock-blue waters are shallow, safe for children, warm, and inviting.

5 Playa Esmeralda, Guardalavaca
MAP P4

Lying on the indented Atlantic coastline of Holguín province, Emerald Beach is truly a jewel. When you tire of the sands, wander along the ecological trails that lead through a mangrove and dry forest preserve, or take in the local sights.

6 Playa de los Flamencos, Cayo Coco

One of the most beautiful beaches in the country, Playa de los Flamencos

Playa de los Flamencos

boasts white sand and turquoise waters protected by an offshore coral reef. With half a dozen large, beach-front hotels, the facilities here continue to expand as new hotels are added. However, there is plenty of wilderness as well. Wildlife, including the flamingos from whom the beach gets its name, parade around the inshore lagoons (see p24).

7 Playa Ancón
MAP H4

Shaded by Australian pine, this white-sand beach lying along the Ancón Peninsula is within a 20-minute drive of Trinidad (see p20). The Cuban government is in the process of gradually developing it as a tourist resort and now three all-inclusive hotels and a diving school are found here. The Caribbean seas offer superb snorkeling and diving, but swimmers need to watch out for the microscopic

sea lice that sometimes infest the waters and can result in the occurrence of flu-like infections.

8 Playa Pilar, Cayo Guillermo
MAP K1

Brushed by near-constant breezes, the white sands of this beach are swept into dunes overlooking pristine reef-protected waters, where you can wade knee-deep for 400 yards (366 m). Water birds can be found in the lagoons and mangroves, as well as hungry mosquitoes.

9 Playa Periquillo, Cayo Santa María
MAP J1

A long *pedraplén* (causeway) arcs across a shallow lagoon to reach the low-lying Playa Periquillo bay. The slender beach has pure white sands and warm waters. The shallows offer excellent bonefishing, while coral reefs and a wreckage are perfect for diving enthusiasts.

10 Playa Siboney
MAP P6

The pebbly gray sand here may not be the finest in Cuba, but the setting is lovely. Playa Siboney is one of few places where you can properly interact with locals and enjoy the rhythm of the salsa with them. Accommodation is offered in Caribbean wooden houses.

Playa Ancón's magnificent 2.5-mile (4-km) sweep of white sand

TOP 10 Children's Attractions

Steam train

1 Steam Train Rides
Once a vital resource for hauling sugarcane, many of Cuba's steam trains are now retired as museum pieces. Others are used for excursions at Central Australia (see p19) and at the Museo de Azúcar in Morón. Kids can also whistle down the tracks on a 1907 "choo-choo" that circles Havana's Parque Lenin in the summer months.

2 Cueva del Indio
MAP B2 ■ Carretera Puerto Esperanza, km 36 ■ (48) 77 8053 ■ Open 9am–5pm ■ Adm
This underground cavern in the Valle de San Vicente will delight children with its spooky, bat-ridden stalagmites and stalactites. The main thrill is a boat ride on an underground river that emerges into open air. Horseback rides are also offered (see p17).

3 Acuario Nacional
MAP F5 ■ Avenida 3ra & Calle 62, Miramar, Havana ■ 7202 5871 ■ Open 10am–6pm Tue–Sun ■ Adm
The outdoor National Aquarium in Havana features a large number of mammals, reptiles, birds, and fish.

4 Crocodile Farms
Kids can safely get close to Cuba's endemic crocodile in breeding farms found on the island (see p88). This monster grows to 16 ft (5 m) long. Younger crocodiles are kept apart. Some farms also breed the American crocodile.

5 Cuban Schools
Most Cuban schools are small and intimate, and foreign children are almost always welcomed for brief visits. Local kids are usually curious to learn about foreign cultures. Make arrangements to visit in advance.

6 Valle de la Prehistoria, Santiago de Cuba
Huge *Tyrannosaurus rex* occupy this prehistoric theme park, featuring life-size concrete reptiles. A natural science museum has informative displays on local wildlife (see p114).

Valle de la Prehistoria, Santiago de Cuba

7 Horse-Drawn Carriages
MAP F2 ▪ Parque Josone,
Avenida 1ra, Varadero

Enjoy the sights of La Habana Vieja
or Varadero aboard an elegant
horse-drawn carriage as it clip-clops
through cobbled streets.

8 El Morro, Santiago de Cuba
This ancient castle with impressive
clifftop battlements comes alive at
dusk, with a daily ceremony that
sees real-life members of the Cuban
military, dressed in the costumes of
Independence soldiers, marching
into the castle to fire a ceremonial
cannon. The castle also displays a
fine collection of muskets, swords,
and other armaments from
yesteryear *(see p30)*.

Remedios amusement park

9 Amusement Parks
MAP F2 ▪ Todo en Uno:
Autopista Sur & Calle 54, Varadero
▪ Open 6–11pm Tue–Thu, 11am–
11pm Fri–Sun ▪ Adm

Nearly every Cuban town has a *parque
de diversiones*. Todo en Uno in
Varadero has modern rides that
include *carros locos* (bumper cars)
and a roller coaster. Havana's main
amusement park is in Parque Lenin.

10 Baseball
Estadio Latinoamericano: Calle
Consejero Arango & Pedro Pérez,
Cerro, Havana ▪ 7879 5952

Older children will enjoy the buzz
of an evening baseball game. It is
a spectacle accompanied by lots of
music and cheering, and the games
often end late at night.

TOP 10 ACTIVITIES FOR CHILDREN IN HAVANA

Children in-line skating in Prado

1 Acuario Nacional
Children are enthralled by the sea-lion
enclosures and the tropical species on
display at the National Aquarium.

2 Cañonazo
MAP X1
Soldiers fire a cannon at 9pm every
evening from El Morro fortress.

3 Shadow-puppetry
MAP X5 ▪ Av. del Puerto & Obrapía
▪ 7861 0568
El Arca (The Ark) puppet museum
and theater puts on delightful shows.

4 Horseback Rides
Kids can mount horses in Parque
Lenin or Parque Luz y Caballero, one
block north of Plaza de la Catedral.

5 Planetario
MAP X5 ▪ Plaza Vieja ▪ 7864 9544
A smart tour around the solar system
with hi-tech gadgetry.

6 Playas del Este
These family-friendly beaches outside
Havana have warm waters *(see p54)*.

7 Prado
A great place to interact with Cuban
children who enjoy in-line skating.

8 Teatro Guiñol
MAP U1 ▪ Calle M & 17 ▪ 7832 6262
This theater in Vedado has comedy
and *marioneta* (puppet) shows.

9 Sala de Teatro de la Orden Tercera
MAP W2 ▪ Calle Oficios & Churruca
▪ 7860 7699
La Colmenita children's ensemble
performs here.

10 Trompoloco Circus
Calle 112, Playa ▪ 7206 5608,
7206 5609
Clowns and acrobats perform beneath
a huge circus tent.

TOP 10 Musical Styles

A group of Cuban musicians play *son* in a shaded plaza

1 Son
Son became popular in the second half of the 19th century in the eastern province of Oriente. Its popularity peaked in the 1950s and was revived decades later by the *Buena Vista Social Club* movie and album.

2 Classical
Cuba boasts a National Symphony Orchestra and many smaller accomplished ensembles sponsored by the government. A unique style has evolved, known as *Afrocubanismo*, which incorporates African-derived instruments and rhythms into classical themes.

Cuban jazz performer

3 Jazz
A musical form that has made a resounding comeback in Cuba in recent years, jazz was suppressed following the Revolution *(see p37)*. A fast-paced Afro-Cuban style has emerged, propelling Cuban musicians to the fore of the world jazz scene, and the Havana International Jazz Festival is a major event in the musical calendar.

4 Danzón
Originating in France via Haiti in the 18th century, *danzón* is the root source of most Cuban music, and gained popularity within slave culture and with Creole peasants. Played by *orquestras típicas, danzón* has a repetitive jaunty tempo, and is the Cuban national dance.

5 Changüí
A rougher variant of *son*, *changüí* has minimal instrumentation with the *tres* (similar to a guitar) and *bongos* dominating. It is played mainly in the eastern provinces, notably by groups such as the Estrellas Campesinas and Grupo Changüí.

Brass section of a classical orchestra

6 Guaguancó

Born in the slave *barracoons* of 18th-century sugar estates, this folkloric Afro-Cuban dance is highly flirtatious. Accompanied by complex bongo rhythms, the male dancer circles his female partner, who dances in a provocative yet defensive manner in front of him.

7 Timba

A derivative of salsa, the highly aggressive and innovative *timba* is an eclectic and evolving musical form that incorporates various genres, including classical, disco, and even hip hop. Improvisation is key to this flexible form.

8 Rumba

Social gatherings in Cuba often evolve into informal *rumbas*, a generic term which covers a variety of African-derived rhythms and dances involving sensuous flicks of the hips. Many rumbas involve a call-and-answer pattern between singers and drummers.

Rumba dancers

9 Salsa

A popular form that evolved in the 1960s, when Cuban musicians began experimenting with new sounds and styles from the US. Fusing jazz and rock with traditional *son*, it is normally fast and intense, but can also be slow and romantic.

10 Rap

Cuba's contemporary rap scene differs markedly from its aggressive US counterpart. *Raperos* use rap to express their frustrations and focus on socio-political commentary with the intention of bettering society.

TOP 10 MUSICIANS

Chucho Valdés

1 Chucho Valdés (b.1941)
This Grammy award-winning jazz pianist is considered to be one of the world's greats.

2 Compay Segundo (1907–2003)
Sentimental guitarist of the 1940s, Segundo's career was resurrected with the *Buena Vista Social Club* movie.

3 Frank Fernández (b.1944)
Cuba's foremost classical pianist and composer studied at Moscow's Tchaikovsky Conservatory.

4 Celia Cruz (1925–2003)
Legendary salsa singer who left Cuba in 1960 and found fame in the US.

5 Benny Moré (1919–63)
This tenor sang everything from *son* to *mambo* and is considered perhaps the greatest Cuban singer of all.

6 Juan Formell (1942–2014)
Founder of Orquesta Revé and Los Van Van – Cuba's most popular salsa band.

7 Silvio Rodríguez (b.1946)
The foremost exponent of politicized *nueva trova* ballads, also a former member of parliament.

8 Gonzalo Rubalcaba (b.1963)
This contemporary jazz pianist performs in concerts all over the world and is a Grammy award winner.

9 Pablo Milanés (b.1943)
A singer-songwriter of *nueva trova*, this guitarist hails from the city of Bayamo.

10 Rubén González (1919–2003)
A renowned jazz pianist, González first performed in 1940 and starred in *Buena Vista Social Club*.

📻 Places to Meet the Locals

Locals and tourists alike gather on the white sands of Playas del Este

① Playas del Este
On weekends, families flee sticky Havana for a day at the beach. Tourists usually gather toward the west end, though many Cuban families prefer the beach around Guanabo (see p54).

② Parque Central, Havana
Havana has many plazas, but this tree-shaded park on the edge of Old Havana is the liveliest. Baseball fans gather here to argue the finer points of the game. With plenty of benches, it is a great place to watch the flurry of activity. Expect *jineteros* (hustlers) to approach you to tout their wares or services (see p125).

③ The Malecón, Havana
The cooling breezes of the capital's seafront esplanade attracts *habaneros* (Havana locals) of all ages, who socialize with guitars and bottles of rum. On hot days families bathe in the *balnearios* cut into the limestone rock. It's the perfect place for a sunset stroll but take care and be sure to watch your step – the sidewalk is crumbling and waves often crash right over the seawall (see p14).

④ Casas de la Trova
When bitten by the dancing bug, head to a Casa de la Trova. Every town has one of these traditional live music houses, where Cuban singles as well as couples have a great time dancing to salsa and timeless *sons* and *boleros*.

⑤ Calle Obispo, Havana
This pedestrian-only shopping street has plenty of intriguing shops, bars, cafés, and ice-cream stores. It is also packed with private art galleries (see p80). Pickpockets are on the prowl, so make sure you guard your belongings.

Calle Obispo, Havana

6 Baseball Games

Watching a Cuban baseball game is as much a social experience as a sporting one. The crowds are passionate but friendly, and the game is interspersed with chatting and drinking. You will make new friends here, even if you support the "other" team.

7 Cumbanchas

Few Cubans have money for discos, so they spark up their own song and dance at street parties where anyone can join in. Contribute a bottle of rum, the drink of choice, as courtesy. Even if you arrive with a partner, expect to be asked to dance.

8 Coppelia

Cubans adore ice cream, and every major town has an outlet selling the Coppelia brand. Seating is communal and ice cream is sold in Cuban pesos at incredibly low prices. Standing in line with Cubans is part of the experience. The branch in Havana is spread over an entire block (see p79).

Mercados Agropecuarios, Havana

9 Mercados Agropecuarios

The farmers' markets are packed with Cubans shopping for fresh produce, while others enjoy the local gossip. Every town has at least one "agro." Even if you are not planning to buy, the atmosphere makes a visit worthwhile.

10 Casas de la Cultura

These cultural centers can be found in every town. The atmosphere is informal and they are great places to make new friends and perhaps learn a few dance moves.

TOP 10 CUSTOMS AND BELIEFS

Taking it easy on the Malecón

1 Politeness
Old-fashioned courtesy, such as saying "thank you" and "please," is very important to Cuban people.

2 Dress
Cubans dress fairly conventionally. Anyone wearing alternative clothing may be viewed as anti-establishment.

3 Santería
More than half the Cuban population are followers of this Afro-Cuban religion (see pp48–9).

4 Racial Harmony
Cuba is an ethnically diverse society, and the degree of racial harmony on the island is profound.

5 Equality
The concept of equality for all on every level is a concept Cubans hold very close to their hearts.

6 Take it Easy
Hurrying is uncommon in Cuba, and foreigners who expect things to happen quickly can be disappointed.

7 Greetings
Cubans greet everyone upon entering a room. People refer to each other as *compañero* (companion).

8 Machismo
This is totally ingrained among most men – even married men flirt openly.

9 "The New Man"
Che Guevara dreamed of creating a society where people were motivated by altruism.

10 Chistes (Jokes)
A great sense of humor helps many Cubans deal with the hardships of daily life – the subject of most *chistes*.

𝗧𝗢𝗣𝟭𝟬 Cuban Dishes

Cerdo Asado (succulent roast pork)

1 Cerdo Asado
Pork is roasted in an open oven or on a spit, and is served whole on skewers or sliced. *Cerdo Asado* is usually served with rice and black beans accompanied by fried plantain.

2 Moros y Cristianos
The base of *comida criolla* (traditional Cuban fare), this dish comprises white rice cooked with black beans and is served as an accompaniment to meat and seafood meals. It is known as *congrí* when cooked with red beans and *congrí oriental* when the red and black beans are mixed.

Moros y Cristianos

3 Bistec Uruguayo
"Uruguayan beef," a staple found on many restaurant menus, is a steak stuffed with ham and cheese. It is usually accompanied by a side salad of boiled vegetables, mashed potatoes or rice, and beans. Fish and chicken are often used instead of beef.

4 Corvina al Ajillo
This simple and delicious dish of seabass with a garlic sauce is typically combined with slices of lime and regular vegetables such as carrots. Usually either mashed potatoes or *moros y cristianos* are served on the side.

5 Pollo con Quimbombó
A traditional country recipe, this dish is a chicken casserole simmered with chopped okra, onions, garlic, green pepper, and tomato, plus plantain and seasoned with black pepper, coriander, and lime juice. It is served with a bowl of steamed or boiled *malanga* (a starchy root vegetable), yams, and potatoes, along with white rice.

6 Potaje
Black beans are slow-cooked with garlic, onions, pepper, oregano, and other herbs to produce this delicious, thick soup. Sometimes pieces of pork or chicken are added. A bowl of plain white rice is usually the sole accompaniment.

7 Ajiaco
This minestrone-style vegetable stew is made with *malanga*, turnips, corn, and yucca, plus a variety of meats, including pork and chicken. It is seasoned with herbs.

Ajiaco, a popular Cuban stew

Classic Cuban flan

8 Flan
Cuba's most popular dessert, apart from ice cream, this is found on most menus. It closely resembles *crème caramel*. A sweet custard made from eggs and milk is baked over a caramelized sugar base, which, when the dish is turned out, provides a delicious sauce.

9 Ropa Vieja
The "old rope" is a combination of boiled rice, black beans, fried plantain, and shredded beef marinated in red wine or rum, seasoned with onions, peppers, oregano, and cumin.

Ropa Vieja

10 Enchilado de Langosta
Lobster is typically boiled, then cooked in a sauce of tomatoes and spiced with peppers and other seasonings. Shrimp is often used as a substitute for lobster. It is usually served with rice and a salad of lettuce and boiled vegetables.

TOP 10 DRINKS

Ice-cold mojitos

1 Mojito
This world-famous Cuban drink is made of white rum with mint leaves, sugar, and a dash of soda water.

2 Cuba Libre
Dark rum with cola and natural lime juice served with plenty of ice in a tall glass, garnished with a lime.

3 Cristal
A light, lager-style beer, usually served chilled. It has a milder taste than the more full-bodied Bucanero beer.

4 Rum
Younger "white" rums are used for most cocktails, while aged rums – *uñejos* – are typically drunk straight.

5 Daiquirí
White rum blended with sugar, lime juice, and crushed ice, and served in a broad glass decorated with a maraschino cherry.

6 Fruit Juices
Many tropical fruits are packaged as fresh juices, including *guayaba* (guava), grapefruit, and orange.

7 Batidos
Water or milk is blended with ice and fresh fruit, such as mango and papaya, to make a refreshing shake.

8 Refrescos
An infinite variety of tropical fruit-flavored, water-based, sweetened drinks, often carbonated.

9 Pru
Made from various herbs and roots, this medicinal drink is served in the eastern provinces of Cuba.

10 Chorote
Strongly flavored chocolate drink of Baracoa, thickened with cornstarch and sweetened with sugar.

🔟 Things to Buy

1 Papier-Mâché Models

Cuban artisans are skilled at making papier-mâché items, and pre-revolutionary American automobiles are a very popular theme. These cars can be incredibly lifelike or have comical distortions. Look out as well for papier-mâché *muñequitas* (dolls) of the *orishas*, or figures of baseball players and cigar-smoking *mulattas* (Cuban women of mixed racial heritage).

Painted papier-mâché model cars

2 Guayaberas

This Cuban cotton shirt worn by men is ideal for beating the heat. It features a straight hem and is worn draped outside the trousers. Either long- or short-sleeved, the shirts usually have four buttoned pockets and are embroidered with twin vertical stripes down the front.

3 Wood Carvings

Carved wooden statues are a staple of craft markets found all over Cuba. The most common items,

Wooden carvings at a street market

which make good souvenirs or gifts, are exaggeratedly slender nude female figures made of mahogany, ebony, and *lignum vitae*. Bowls and plates are also available, as are chess sets and humidors, often made in colorful combinations of different types of hardwoods.

4 Fans

Traditional, handmade, and prettily painted Spanish fans or *abanicos* make a great gift. The fans are hand-painted in an age-old tradition. Gift shops throughout Cuba also sell them.

5 Che Guevara T-shirts

Almost every Cuban souvenir store and flea market sells cotton T-shirts for men, women, and children. The most common image is the iconic photo of Che Guevara in his trademark black beret with the five-point revolutionary star.

6 Music CDs

CDs of everything from *son* and jazz to *timba* and salsa are widely available in *casas de la trova* (see p60), souvenir stores, and shops run by the state-owned recording entity EGREM. Musicians who perform at restaurants and other such venues often offer recordings of their music for sale.

7 Coffee

Some of the best mountain-grown beans in the Caribbean are sold in vacuum-sealed packages at reasonable prices. Many shops sell a rich, smooth export-quality brand called Cubanita.

8 Cuban Art

Although much Cuban art is kitsch and mass-produced for tourists, the nation's many artists also produce some of the most visually exciting works in the Caribbean. Colorful recreations of typical street scenes featuring old American automobiles or ox-drawn carts are irresistible, but also look for more profound works by contemporary masters. The former are sold at street markets nationwide; the latter are represented at quality state-run galleries.

Cuban art on display

9 Jewelry

Scour the street markets for creative avant-garde pieces made from recycled cutlery. Black coral finds its way into contemporary silver, and sometimes into gold jewelry sold at state-run *joyerías* (jewelry stores) in Havana. Black coral looks very pretty when set in jewelry, but bear in mind that it is a threatened species.

10 Lace

Much of Cuba's beautiful, traditional lace embroidery is from Trinidad, the center of homespun production. Look for exquisite tablecloths, antimacassars, and blouses, as well as pretty, crocheted bikinis.

TOP 10 RUMS AND CIGARS

1 Havana Club Gran Reserva
Aged for 15 years, this is one of the finest Cuban rums, with a texture and flavor like a superb cognac.

2 Ron Matusalem Añejo
Elegant rum aged in barrels for 10 years, three years longer than most *añejos*.

3 Montecristo No. 4
The world's top-selling cigar; the preferred smoke of Che Guevara.

4 Cohiba Siglo
Large, flawless cigar loaded with flavor.

Cohiba Siglo

5 Varadero Oro
Aged for five years, this dark golden rum is smooth, sweet, and has distinctive caramel flavors.

6 Partagás Series D
A full-bodied cigar with an intense, earthy flavor, this Robusto is the standard-bearer of the Partagás brand.

7 Montecristo Figurados No. 2
This extremely rare, perfectly balanced, distinctly flavored, torpedo-shaped cigar is sought after by connoisseurs.

8 Ron Santiago 45 Aniversario
A limited-edition, well-aged rum with hints of honey and walnuts – one of Cuba's finest.

9 Romeo y Julieta Churchill
This long, large, full-bodied smoke is named after Shakespeare's tragic play and British premier Winston Churchill.

10 Trinidad Fundadores
A classic, considered perhaps the finest of Cuban cigars. Fidel Castro presented these to visiting dignitaries.

Havana Club rum

🔟 Cuba for Free

Catedral de La Habana

1 La Habana Vieja

Havana's greatest freebie happens to be a must-see attraction with a handful of colonial plazas and dozens of bustling streets to explore. Don't miss Catedral de La Habana, the Plaza de Armas (see p72) with its book market, or Parque Central (see p75) – the epicenter of social life – surrounded by astonishing buildings.

2 The Malecón

On any evening, and especially on weekends, Havana's seafront boulevard becomes an impromptu party scene. Thousands of young Cubans sit on the sea wall to watch the sunset, flirt, listen to music, and share bottles of rum. By day you'll find skateboarders, in-line skaters, fishermen, musicians, and always romantic couples (see p76).

3 Beach Resorts

Not all Cuba's beaches are free. Those accessed by *pedraplén* (see p25) charge a fee for use of the causeway. But other scintillating white sands, such as those of Playas del Este (see p54) and Varadero, are free, and there's never a charge for enjoying the warm turquoise seas.

4 Churches

Although most museums have an admission charge, Cuba is replete with ancient churches that are free to enter and enjoy, such as the exquisite Baroque Catedral de La Habana (see p73), and the Basílica de Nuestra de Señora de la Caridad del Cobre (see p113), just outside Santiago de Cuba.

5 Casa de la Trovas

Every town has a traditional music house where you can enjoy live music and dance to your heart's content. Many offer afternoon as well as evening activities, usually free of charge. It's a great way to strike up friendships with Cubans (see p60). The best casas are those in Trinidad and Santiago de Cuba (see p115).

6 Colonial Trinidad

Simply strolling the cobbled streets of this colonial gem will immerse you in a quintessential Cuban experience (see pp20–21). Dozens of private art galleries line the plazas, and the Iglesia Parroquial de la Santísima Trinidad (see p106) can be enjoyed for free, as can such nearby attractions as the Valle de los Ingenios (see p103), with its fascinating ruined sugar mills.

Iznaga Tower, Valle de los Ingenios

7 Plaza de la Revolución

Although there's a fee for the museum beneath the giant monument to National Hero José Martí, this massive plaza (see p74) in the heart of Havana is surrounded by impressive sights, including the giant steel mural of Che Guevara that dominates the Ministerio del Interior. A convertible classic car taxi is the most atmospheric and stylish way to arrive in the plaza, but the Havana BusTour also stops here (see pp120–21).

Steel mural in Plaza de la Revolución

8 Free Festivals

Fancy mingling with locals at one of the many annual festivals (see pp68–9) in Cuba? You can let your hair down in the revelry of Carnaval in Santiago de Cuba; enjoy the thrilling firework spectacle of Remedios' year-end *parranda*; or even show solidarity during the Día de los Trabajadores (Day of the Workers).

9 Casas de la Cultura

Meet local artists, musicians, poets, and writers in community centers known as Casas de la Cultura, found all over the country (see p61). Enjoy cultural activities such as live performances, music shows, art exhibitions, and dance classes – almost everything they put on is free.

10 Bandstands

Most big towns in Cuba have a central square with bandstands, where local bands perform for free, usually on weekend nights. Sit on a bench or grab someone's hand and join the locals in these wonderful expressions of community spirit.

TOP 10 MONEY-SAVING TIPS

Casa particular **interior**

1 Havana BusTour takes in most of Havana's top sights for the price of a single all-day fare. With 41 stops along the route, it really is a complete sightseeing experience.

2 Take advantage of the good-value set *cajita* lunches that are sold at roadside stalls.

3 Stay at *casas particulares*, which offer great value and give you insight into how Cuban families live.

4 Join the Cubans in line at Coppelia and pay for your ice cream in pesos, rather than standing in the more expensive CUC$ line. Most large cities have a Coppelia outlet.

5 Buy a ticket for both sections of the Museo de Bellas Artes, as the Cuban and International sections charge more if you pay separately.

6 Rather than taking relatively expensive taxis, travel by public bus or hop into a *colectivo* taxi for longer journeys within cities.

7 Comb through the book fair at Havana's Plaza de Armas for rare posters and other unique retro finds (see p72).

8 When exchanging foreign currency, avoid using US dollars, which are subject to a 10 percent surcharge.

9 Go gallery-hopping in Trinidad, where dozens of roadside stores sell artwork of surprisingly good quality.

10 Watch for special two-for-one offers on telephone cards for public phones; avoid using expensive hotel phones.

🔟 Festivals and Holidays

1 Jan 1, Liberation Day

New Year's Day in Cuba is celebrated as the day that dictator Fulgencio Batista (see p43) was toppled. Officially known as the "Anniversary of the Triumph of the Revolution," the event is marked by nationwide musical concerts.

2 Jan 28, José Martí's Birthday

Cubans celebrate the birth of their national hero (see p37) with events including readings of Martí's poetry and concerts. Children are integral to the celebrations.

Children on José Martí's birthday

3 Apr 19, Victoria de Playa Girón

The plaza and museum behind the beach at Playa Girón is the setting for speeches, a wreath-laying ceremony, and festivities to celebrate the "first defeat of imperialism in the Americas." The holiday honors the Cuban victory in the Bay of Pigs invasion (see p37).

4 May 1, Día de los Trabajadores

As many as half a million citizens march through Plaza de la Revolución (see p15), while Cuba's leaders look on. Rallies that include the singing of patriotic songs are held throughout the island, as Cubans proclaim their dedication to socialism and the Revolution.

5 Jul 26, National Revolution Day

A celebration of the launch of the Revolution of 1953 (see p37) is held in a different city each year. Attendees dress in black and red T-shirts – the colors of Castro's revolutionary movement – and listen to speeches by Communist leaders.

6 Jul, Carnaval

Many major cities organize a street carnival in July featuring live music and dancing. The biggest event is in Santiago de Cuba (see pp30–31), where carnival season climaxes with a parade of bands along Avenida Jesús Menéndez.

Revellers celebrating the Día de los Trabajadores

7 Oct 8, Anniversary of Che Guevara's death

Santa Clara's Plaza de la Revolución and the Monumento del Che *(see p39)* are the setting for a wreath-laying ceremony in the presence of key political leaders.

8 Oct 28, Memorial to Camilo Cienfuegos

Schoolchildren in Havana march to the Malecón *(see p14)* to throw "a flower for Camilo" into the sea on the anniversary of the death of Cienfuegos *(see p41)*. This revolutionary commander went missing in 1959, when his plane disappeared during a night flight. There is also a parade to the sea at the Museo de Camilo Cienfuegos in Jaguajay, Sancti Spíritus province.

Ballet Nacional de Cuba

9 Nov, Festival de Ballet

For 10 days biennially at the end of October, Havana's Gran Teatro *(see p77)* plays host to brilliant ballet performances featuring leading international dancers and ballet corps. Hosted by the Ballet Nacional de Cuba, the festival is one of the major events in the cultural calendar.

10 Dec, Festival de Nuevo Cine Latinoamericano

Cubans are avid moviegoers, and the highlight of their year is the Latin American Film Festival, which screens a variety of art-house films and documentaries from around the world, as well as works from some of Cuba's own top directors.

TOP 10 LOCAL FESTIVALS

Parrandas in Remedios

1 Holguín (Jan), Semana de Cultura Holguinera
The town comes alive with a medley of cultural activities.

2 Camagüey (Feb), Jornadas de la Cultura Camagüeyana
This city celebrates its founding with much fanfare.

3 Trinidad (Easter), El Recorrido del Vía Cruce
Catholic devotees follow the ancient "way of the cross."

4 Las Tunas (Jun), Jornada Cucalambeana
Singers compete in *décimas* – ten-syllable rhyming verses – to honor this composer.

5 Cienfuegos (Aug), Festival Internacional Benny Moré
Celebrated every other year to honor Benny Moré *(see p59)*.

6 Santiago de Cuba (Aug), Festival de Pregón
Citizens converge on Parque Céspedes to recite traditional songs and verses.

7 Guantánamo (Dec), Festival del Changüí
An excuse to party as *son* groups perform *(see p58)*.

8 Trinidad (Dec), Fiestas Navideñas
The journey of Mary and Joseph is re-created.

9 Rincón (Dec 17), Procesión de los Milagros
The *orisha* St Lazarus is honored in this pilgrimage.

10 Remedios (24–29 Dec), Parrandas
Two sides of town duel in a firework contest *(see p95)*.

Cuba
Area by Area

Musicians in Trinidad

🔟 Havana

From the colonial splendor of La Habana Vieja (Old Havana) to the early 20th-century grandeur of Vedado, central Havana is full of appeal. Centered on four colonial plazas, much of La Habana Vieja

Street sign

has been restored and teems with atmospheric hotels, top restaurants, trendy boutiques, and hip bars. Vedado's grid of tree-shaded streets is lined with once-resplendent mansions. Attractions here include the Plaza de la Revolución, the setting for political marches past and present. Nightclubs from the area's 1950s heyday still sizzle, and high-rise hotels of the same era remain a popular draw.

① Plaza de Armas
MAP X4 ■ El Templete: open 9am–5pm Tue–Sat (to 1pm Sun); adm

This cobbled plaza (see p13), laid out in 1582 as the administrative center of Cuba, is named for the military exercises that took place here. It is

surrounded by notable buildings, such as the Castillo de la Real Fuerza (see p47), the temple-like Neo-Classical El Templete, and the Palacio de los Capitanes Generales – a former governor's palace housing Museo de la Ciudad (see p46).

AREA MAP OF HAVANA

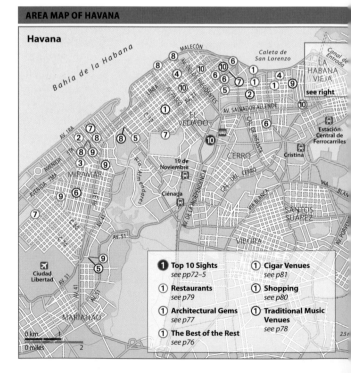

❶ Top 10 Sights	❶ Cigar Venues
see pp72–5	see p81
❶ Restaurants	❶ Shopping
see p79	see p80
❶ Architectural Gems	❶ Traditional Music
see p77	Venues
❶ The Best of the Rest	see p78
see p76	

Colonial mansions surround the Catedral de La Habana

② Catedral de La Habana

Havana's charming cathedral (1777), officially known as Catedral de la Virgen María de la Concepción Inmaculada and sometimes referred to as Catedral San Cristóbal, has an exquisite Baroque facade supported by pilasters and asymmetrical bell towers. Restored frescoes by Giuseppe Perovani adorn the relatively austere altar. The plaza on which the cathedral stands is surrounded by colonial mansions (see p12).

③ Plaza Vieja

MAP X5 ■ Fototeca de Cuba: Calle Mercaderes 307; 7862 2530; open 10am–5pm Tue–Sat ■ Museo de Naipes: 7860 1534; open 9:30am–5pm Tue–Sat, 9am–2:30pm Sun; adm

Magnificent buildings spanning four centuries rise on each side of this square (see p12). The 18th-century building housing the Fototeca de Cuba has photography exhibitions; the Museo de Naipes displays a collection of playing cards.

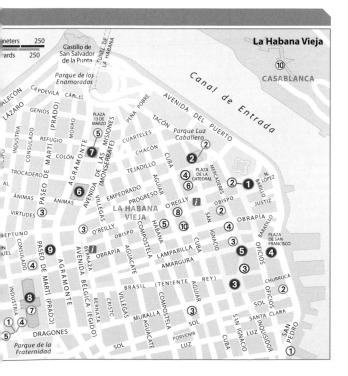

4 Plaza de San Francisco

This cobbled plaza formerly opened onto the harborfront. It is dominated by the Basilica Menor de San Francisco de Asís – a former cathedral that ceased to be used for worship following British occupation in 1762. Today it is a concert hall as well as a religious art museum. The plaza also features an eclectic array of restored buildings spanning three centuries (see p12).

5 Calle Mercaderes

MAP X5 ■ Casa de Asia: Calle Mercaderes 111, La Habana Vieja; 7863 9740; open 9am–5pm Tue–Sat, 9am–noon Sun ■ Museo del Tabaco: Calle Mercaderes 120, La Habana Vieja; 7861 5795; open 10am–5pm Tue–Sat, 9am– 1pm Sun; adm ■ Maqueta de La Habana: Calle Mercaderes 114, La Habana Vieja; 7866 4425; open 9am–5pm Tue–Sat (to 12:30pm Sun); adm

This cobbled street (see p12) is lined with colonial mansions housing tiny museums, boutiques, and other fascinating places. The three blocks might take a full morning to explore, with requisite stops at the Museo de Asia, Museo del Tabaco, and Maqueta de La Habana – a fabulous scale-model of La Habana Vieja. Break your stroll at Mesón de la Flota, a *bodega* hosting live flamenco.

6 Museo Nacional de Bellas Artes

This world-class museum is in two parts. An international section occupies the Renaissance-style Centro Asturiano, built in 1927, and boasts treasures from Ancient Egypt, Greece, and Rome. There are also

RESTORING OLD HAVANA

In 1982, UNESCO recognized La Habana Vieja (**below**) as a World Heritage Site, and Cuba initiated a plan to save the crumbling colonial city. Eusebio Leal, the Havana City Historian, has overseen the remarkable effort. Priority has been given to the most important buildings, many of which have been transformed into museums, hotels, and bars.

works by North American and European masters, including Gainsborough, Goya, and Rubens. The Modernist Palace of Fine Arts, a separate building two blocks away, displays works by Cuban artists from different periods (see p12).

7 Plaza de la Revolución

The administrative and political center of Cuba since the early 1950s, the plaza is surrounded with Modernist and monumentalist government buildings. Huge political rallies are held here. The Memorial José Martí on the south side features a large granite monument to the national hero, plus an excellent museum topped by a Surrealist tower. A striking visage of Che Guevara adorns the facade of the Ministerio del Interior (see p15).

Museum within the Memorial José Martí in Plaza de la Revolución

8 Capitolio

The nation's grandiose former congressional building was inaugurated in 1929 and incorporates Art Deco elements into a Neo-Classical design that closely resembles Washington D. C.'s Capitol. It is undergoing a lengthy restoration and will host the National Assembly. Visitors approach via a steep flight of stairs flanked by Neo-Classical bronze figures. Behind the central portico with its 12 granite columns are three bronze doors with bas-reliefs of major events of Cuban history. A huge Statue of the Republic stands at the entrance hall, which features a fake 25-carat diamond embedded in the floor (see p14).

The grand Capitolio building

9 Parque Central

An epicenter of social life in Havana, this palm-shaded square has a statue of José Martí (see p42) and is surrounded by monumental 19th- and 20th-century buildings. These include the Neo-Classical Hotel Plaza and the spectacular Gran Teatro (see p77).

10 Museo de la Revolución

Housed in the former presidential palace once occupied by General Batista, this museum (see p13) is a tribute to the Revolution, from the guerrilla war to the current day. The ornate, domed building, built in 1920, is as fascinating as the collection, and includes the Salón de los Espejos, a hall lined with mirrors. At the rear is the Granma Memorial (see p.38), featuring the yacht Granma as well as aircrafts and vehicles used in the Bay of Pigs invasion (see p37).

LA HABANA VIEJA WALK

[Map diagram with the following labels:]
Catedral — Plaza de la Catedral — Castillo de la Real Fuerza
La Bodeguita del Medio
Palacio de los Capitanes Generales
Plaza de Armas
Basílica Menor de San Francisco de Asís
La Imprenta
Factoría Plaza Vieja — Plaza Vieja

▶ MORNING

After breakfast, head to **Plaza de la Catedral** (see p12), the most intimate of the city's colonial plazas. Peek inside the **Catedral de La Habana** and then stop for a drink at Ernest Hemingway's favorite haunt, **La Bodeguita del Medio** (see p78). Admire the locals in their colonial dresses before strolling along Calle San Ignacio, with its art galleries. Then turn left on Calle O'Reilly and walk two blocks south to **Plaza de Armas** (see p13). Move around the square in a clockwise direction, stopping to admire the **Castillo de la Real Fuerza** (see p47). On the park's eastern side, explore the **Palacio de los Capitanes Generales** (see p12), before exiting the square along Calle Oficios. Take your time to admire the 18th-century buildings here.

AFTERNOON

Stop for refreshments at **La Imprenta**, a stylish restaurant on cobbled Calle Mercaderes. Revived, continue southeast to visit the **Basílica Menor de San Francisco de Asís**, where you can scale the bell tower for great views over the harbor and La Habana Vieja. Then walk toward **Plaza Vieja** (see p73), where highlights include the Museo de Naipes and the Cámara Oscura, a rooftop optical reflection camera that offers a magnified view of life from the top of Havana. End your day with a meal and chilled beer at **Factoría Plaza Vieja**, a brewpub on the plaza.

See map on pp72–3 ←

The Best of the Rest

 Malecón
MAP S2–W1

Connecting La Habana Vieja to Vedado, this seafront boulevard offers grand vistas and is a gathering spot for locals. Beware of dangerous potholes.

 Fundación Havana Club
MAP T3 ▪ Calle San Pedro 262, La Habana Vieja ▪ 7861 8051 ▪ Open 9am–5:30pm Mon–Thu, (to 4pm Fri–Sun) ▪ Adm (includes guided tour and drinks)

The Havana Club Foundation's lively museum educates visitors on rum production. A range of rums can be sampled at the bar.

3 Paseo de Martí
Known locally as "Prado," this is a is a tree-shaded promenade guarded by bronze lions. Here, children play improptu soccer matches as locals sit and chat (see p14).

4 Fábrica de Tabacos H. Upmann
MAP V2 ▪ Calle Belascoaín 852, Centro Habana ▪ 7878 1059 ▪ Open 9am–5pm Mon–Fri ▪ Adm for guided tours (book in advance through a state tour agent)

This cigar factory dates back to 1875 and provides a fascinating glimpse into the art of cigar-making.

5 Universidad de La Habana
The city's university boasts Neo-Classical buildings, two museums, and a staircase that was the setting for several violent demonstrations in pre-revolutionary days (see p14).

6 Hotel Nacional
MAP U1 ▪ Calle O & 21 ▪ 7836 3564

This imposing Neo-Classical 1930s hotel draws visitors with its lavish decor, various bars, and gardens.

7 Cementerio Colón
MAP S3–T3 ▪ Av. Zapata & Calle 12, Vedado ▪ 7830 4517 ▪ Open 8am–5pm daily ▪ Adm

One of the world's most astounding cemeteries, this massive necropolis features tombs representing a pantheon of important figures.

8 Miramar
The most elegant district of Havana, Miramar's leafy avenues are lined with grandiose mansions. Many modern deluxe hotels are here.

9 Museo Ernest Hemingway
MAP V3 ▪ Calle Vigía, San Francisco de Paula ▪ 7692 0176 ▪ Open 10am–4:30pm Mon–Sat (closed when raining) ▪ Adm ▪ mushem@cubarte. cult.cu

Hemingway's former home remains just as he left it (see p47).

10 Parque Histórico-Militar Morro-Cabaña
MAP X1 ▪ Carretera de la Cabaña ▪ 7791 1222 ▪ Open 9am–6pm daily (El Morro); 9am–10pm (San Carlos de la Cabaña) ▪ Adm

This vast military complex comprises El Morro castle and the Fortaleza de San Carlos de la Cabaña, the largest fortress in the Americas.

Fortaleza de San Carlos de la Cabaña

Architectural Gems

1 Edificio Solimar

MAP V1 ■ Calle Soledad 205, Centro Habana

This remarkable Art Deco apartment complex has curvaceous balconies that wrap around the building.

2 Catedral de La Habana
The Baroque facade of this 18th-century church is adorned with pilasters and flanked by asymmetrical bell towers, one thinner than the other *(see p12)*.

3 Edificio Bacardí

MAP W5 ■ Av. Monserrate 261, La Habana Vieja

A stunning example of Art Deco, this soaring, multi-tiered edifice has a facade of pink granite and local limestone. The famous Bacardí bat tops a ziggurat bell tower.

4 Gran Teatro
MAP V5 ■ Paseo de Martí 452 ■ 7861 3079 ■ Open 9am–5pm Mon–Sat, 9am–1pm Sun ■ Adm; extra charge for guided tour

This theater, built in 1837, is a Neo-Baroque confection with corner towers topped by angels. It also features sculptures of the muses Charity, Education, Music, and Theater.

5 Palacio Presidencial
MAP W1 ■ Calle Refugio 1

The lavish former presidential palace was intended to signify pomp. It now houses the Museo de la Revolución. The extravagant three-story building is topped by a dome and decorated inside with frescoes and mirrors.

6 Hotel Habana Libre

MAP U1 ■ Calle L & 23

Dominating the Vedado skyline, this oblong Modernist tower, built in 1958, features a dramatic atrium lobby, and a huge mural on its exterior by Amelia Peláez *(see p42)*.

The Capitolio's grand entrance hall

7 Capitolio
This grandiose congressional building is topped by a dome. Its highlight is the sumptuous Salón de los Pasos Perdidos – the entrance hall, with marble floor and gilded lamps *(see p14)*.

8 Casa de las Américas
MAP T1 ■ Calle 3ra & Av. de los Presidentes ■ 7838 2707 ■ Open 10am–4pm Mon–Fri, for events Sat ■ www.casa.cult.cu

Resembling a vertical banded church, this Art Deco building features a triple-tiered clock-tower.

Gran Teatro

9 Tropicana
MAP D2 ■ Calle 72 & Av. del Ferrocarril, Marianao ■ 7267 1717 ■ Open from 8:30pm daily ■ www.cabaret-tropicana.com

Built around trees and considered the masterpiece of Cuban architect Max Borges Recio, this open-air theater is a superb example of 1950s *modernismo*.

10 Instituto Superior de Arte
MAP D2 ■ Calle 120 & 9na, Playa ■ 7208 0705 ■ Open by appointment

Designed by three "rebel" architects, this arts school was never completed, as it was considered too avant-garde.

See map on pp72–3 ←

Traditional Music Venues

1 Sábado de la Rumba
MAP S2 ■ Calle 4 103, Vedado ■ 7830 3060 ■ Open 3pm Sat ■ Adm

Cuba's premier Afro-Cuban dance troupe puts on a spellbinding performance, as the beat draws people to the dance floor.

2 Palacio de la Rumba
MAP U2 ■ Calle San Miguel 860, Centro Habana ■ 7873 0990 ■ Open from 9pm daily ■ Adm

Groups such as the kings of rumba, Los Muñequitos de Matanzas, play to a packed house here. Listings are posted in the window of the venue.

3 Café Taberna
MAP X5 ■ Calle Mercaderes 531, La Habana Vieja ■ 7861 1637 ■ Open noon–11pm daily ■ Adm for shows

Occupying a restored 18th-century mansion, this restaurant has a house band that performs hits from yesteryear.

4 La Bodeguita del Medio
MAP W4 ■ Calle Empedrado 207, La Habana Vieja ■ 7867 1374 ■ Open 10:30am–11:30pm daily

Troubadors play non-stop at this legendary and popular venue, famous for its mojitos and associations with Ernest Hemingway.

5 Tropicana
This sensational cabaret, billed as "Paradise Under the Stars," is held in an open-air auditorium, where scantily clad showgirls in fanciful, ruffled costumes parade under the treetops (see p77).

6 Sangri-La
MAP F5 ■ Calle 42 esq. 21, Miramar ■ 5264 8343 ■ Open noon–3am daily ■ Adm

One of Havana's sizzling hot new private nightclubs, it feels like a piece of Miami in Cuba.

7 La Zorra y El Cuervo
MAP U1 ■ Ave 23, Vedado ■ 7833 2402 ■ Open 10pm–2am ■ Adm

Top-ranked artists play at what is considered to be Havana's premier jazz club. Its name translates as "the fox and the crow."

8 Fabrica de Arte
MAP S2 ■ Calle 26 esq 11, Vedado ■ 7838 2260 ■ Open 8pm–3am Thu–Sun ■ Adm

This hip, new multimedia bar, gallery, and event venue has a New York vibe and an ever-changing menu of live performances.

9 Casa de la Música
MAP V2 ■ Av. Galiano 235, Centro Habana ■ 7862 4165 ■ Open 4–7pm, 10pm–2am daily ■ Adm

Hugely popular with Cubans, this is a great place for salsa music. It has excellent afternoon dance matinees.

Costumed performers at Tropicana

10 Salón Rojo
MAP U1 ■ Calle 21 e/ N y O, Vedado ■ 7833 0666 ■ Open 10pm–4am Wed–Sun ■ Adm

Considered to be Havana's top salsa venue, this sizzling red-themed dance club in the upscale Hotel Capri hosts big-name groups, such as Buena Fe and Los Van Van. It is best to arrive after midnight.

Restaurants

The nostalgic interior of La Gaurida

1 La Guarida
MAP V1 ■ Calle Concordia 418,
Centro Habana ■ 7866 9047
■ $$$ ■ Reservations essential

Superb bohemian ambience, French-
inspired cuisine, and a one-of-a-kind
setting make this the best *paladar*
(see p126) in Cuba.

2 El Tocoroco
MAP F5 ■ Av. 3 & Calle 18,
Miramar ■ 7204 2209 ■ $$$

An extensive menu is on offer in this
quirky dining room decorated with
a fountain, Tiffany lamps, fish tanks,
and wooden toucans.

3 El Aljibe
MAP F5 ■ Av. 7ma & 24,
Miramar ■ 7204 1583 ■ $$

This busy thatched restaurant
serves signature all-you-can-eat
roast chicken with extras. The well-
trained staff are always on their toes.

4 Casa Miglis
MAP V1 ■ Calle Lealtad 120,
Centro Habana ■ 7963 1483 ■ $$

In the renovated ground floor of a
run-down town-house tenement,
this offers exciting avant-garde decor
and delicious *nouvelle* Cuban cuisine.

5 El Cocinero
MAP T2 ■ Calle 26 between 11
& 13, Vedado ■ 7832 2355 ■ $$

Housed in a former cooking-oil
factory, this elegant restaurant
includes an open-air rooftop tapas
bar. Food and service are excellent.

6 Coppelia
MAP U1 ■ Calle L & Ave 23,
Vedado ■ 7831 9908 ■ $

Lose yourself in the many creamy
flavors of Coppelia, touted as the
world's largest ice-cream chain.
This particular branch has two
stories and several open-air parks.

7 El Corte di Principe
MAP F5 ■ Av. 9na & Calle 76,
Miramar ■ 5255 9091 ■ $$

Delicious Italian fare prepared and
served alfresco by the owner, Sergio.
A popular choice is the beef carpaccio.

8 La Chucheria
MAP T1 ■ Calle 1ra e/ C & D,
Vedado ■ 7830 0708 ■ Open 8:30am–
midnight daily ■ $

The current "in" spot at which to
enjoy pizzas alfresco is this retro-
style sports bar-cum-café facing
the Malecón. A second outlet has
opened in Miramar.

9 Cocina de Lilliam
MAP F5 ■ Calle 48 1311,
Miramar ■ 7209 6514 ■ $$

Lilliam, the owner, whips up creative
Cuban dishes, such as lobster with
pineapple, and ice creams in unusual
flavors. You can choose to eat in the
air-conditioned interior or in the
charming garden with fairy-lights.

10 Le Chansonnier
MAP T1 ■ Calle J e/Líne A & 15,
Vedado ■ 7832 1576 ■ $$

French-Cuban partners have created
an elegant *paladar* set within a 1920s
town house. Dramatic decor, superb
French-inspired Cuban dishes, and
excellent service combine for a top-
quality dining experience.

See map on pp72–3 ←

Shopping

1 Centro Cultural Antiguos Almacenes de Depósito San José

MAP X6 ■ Av. Desamparados & San Ignacio, La Habana Vieja ■ 7864 7793

This handsomely restored waterside warehouse on the edge of the Old City is home to Havana's largest artisan market.

2 Second-Hand Book Market

MAP X4 ■ Plaza de Armas, La Habana Vieja

Bibliophiles and bargain-hunters should browse the stalls in Plaza de Armas for books, maps, coins, memorabilia of the Revolution, and curios.

Second-hand books, Plaza de Armas

3 Tienda El Soldadito de Plomo

MAP X5 ■ Calle Muralla 164, La Habana Vieja ■ 7866 0232

An unusual shop where you can buy tiny lead soldiers made on site as well as miniatures of famous characters such as Charlie Chaplin.

4 Havana 1791

MAP X5 ■ Calle Mercaderes 156, La Habana Vieja ■ 7861 3525

This charming perfume store sells brand-name imported perfumes as well as 12 local floral fragrances, made on the premises.

5 El Quitrín

MAP X5 ■ Calle Obispo 163, La Habana Vieja ■ 7862 0810

Find hand-embroidered lace blouses and skirts for ladies and traditional *guayabera* shirts for men.

Taller Experimental de la Gráfica

6 Taller Experimental de la Gráfica

MAP X4 ■ Callejón del Chorro, Plaza de la Catedral, La Habana Vieja ■ 7864 7622

This is the place to buy unique, limited-edition prints hot off the press. You can select from a vast collection of lithographs.

7 Joyería La Habanera

MAP D2 ■ Calle 12 505, Miramar ■ 7204 2546

Items of antique jewelry are available here, as well as funky contemporary pieces using recycled silverware and black coral.

8 Calle Obispo

MAP W5–X4 ■ Calle Obispo, La Habana Vieja

This pedestrian-only street bustles with shoppers browsing bookstores, fashion boutiques, and art galleries, including the large and well-stocked Galería Forma.

9 Casa de la Música EGREM

MAP D2 ■ Calle 20 3309, Miramar ■ 7204 0447 ■ www.egrem.com.cu

EGREM, the state recording company, has the largest selection of music CDs, DVDs, and cassettes in town. Prices, however, are not cheap.

10 Casa del Abanico

MAP W5 ■ Calle Obrapía 107 ■ 7863 4452

Shop here for quality hand-crafted and intricately painted traditional Spanish *abanicos* (fans).

Cigar Venues

1 Salón Cuaba

MAP V5 ▪ Hotel Parque Central, Calle Neptuno & Zulueta ▪ 7860 6627 ▪ Open 9am–6pm daily

Salón Cuaba caters to serious smokers with an elegant smoking lounge and service bar. The staff are knowledgeable.

2 Museo del Tabaco

MAP X5 ▪ Calle Mercaderes 120, La Habana Vieja ▪ 7861 5795 ▪ Open 9am–5pm Tue–Sat (to 1pm Sun)

Displaying paraphernalia relating to smoking, this small museum has a cigar shop downstairs.

3 Hostal Conde de Villanueva

MAP X5 ▪ Calle Mercaderes 202, La Habana Vieja ▪ 7862 9293 ▪ Open 10am–7pm

The sumptuous lounge and excellent service make this a great place to sample cigars.

4 VIPHavana

MAP G5 ▪ Calle 5na 454, Vedado ▪ 7832 0178 ▪ Open noon–3am daily

Havana's expats and Cuba's own cigar-loving VIPs are the most frequent visitors to this hip bar.

Fábrica de Tabacos Partagás

5 Fábrica de Tabacos Partagás

MAP W2 ▪ Calle Industria 520, Centro Habana ▪ 7866 8060 ▪ Closed for renovation

See fine cigars being rolled in a well-stocked humidor, with a VIP room open by invitation.

6 Fábrica de Tabacos H. Upmann

This famous cigar factory was opened in 1875 by the banker Herman Upmann after he moved to Cuba from Germany. It offers factory tours and stocks a wide range of cigars (see p76).

Fábrica de Tabacos H. Upmann

7 Festival del Habano

February ▪ www.habanos.com

Attracting celebrities and cigar-lovers, this festival features concerts and a grand finale auction with humidors signed by Fidel Castro.

8 Club Habana

MAP D2 ▪ 5ta Av. 188/192, Playa ▪ 7275 0390 ▪ Open 9am–11pm

Within a private members' club, this excellent store and lounge is open to the public via a day pass.

9 Casa del Habano

MAP D2 ▪ 5ta Av. & Calle 16, Miramar ▪ 7204 7974 ▪ Open 10am–9pm daily

An upscale store with a huge humidor stocked with the finest brands. Smoke in comfort in the lounge and bar.

10 Fábrica de Tabacos El Laguito

MAP F5 ▪ Av. 146 2302, Cubanacán ▪ 7208 2218 ▪ By appointment

Aficionados who prefer robust Cohibas, Cuba's flagship brand, may want to buy them at the factory where they're made. The Trinidad label is also hand-rolled here.

See map on pp72–3

🔟 Western Cuba

Western Cuba boasts some of the loveliest scenery in the country. The dramatic beauty reaches its pinnacle in the Valle de Viñales in Pinar del Río. These mountains are laced with hiking trails, notably at the mountain communities of Soroa and Las Terrazas, and in the Guanahacabibes Peninsula, at the western tip of Cuba. Fine tobacco is grown in fields tucked into valleys and spread throughout the Vuelta Abajo region. Just off the mainland is Isla de la Juventud, with an expanse of wild terrain that shelters endemic bird life. Neighboring Cayo Largo, an island in the Archipiélago de los Canarreos, with its white beaches, is a tourist haven.

Hillside orchid garden in Soroa

Cuban orchids

AREA MAP OF WESTERN CUBA

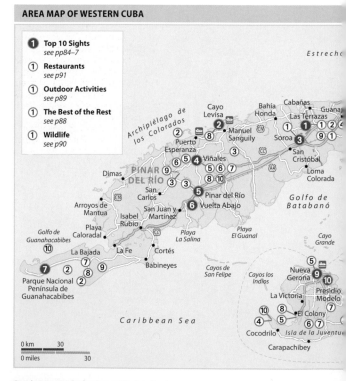

1️⃣ **Top 10 Sights**
see pp84–7

1️⃣ **Restaurants**
see p91

1️⃣ **Outdoor Activities**
see p89

1️⃣ **The Best of the Rest**
see p88

1️⃣ **Wildlife**
see p90

Previous pages Scuba diver in María la Gorda

Lake at Las Terrazas

1 Las Terrazas

MAP C2 ■ Hotel La Moka: Autopista Nacional, km 51, Pinar del Río; (48) 57 8600 ■ www.lasterrazas.cu

Founded in 1968 as a village in the pine-clad mountains of the eastern Sierra del Rosario, this community (see p16) has a lovely setting with simple houses built in terraces overlooking a lake. The local Hotel

La Moka focuses on ecotourism and arranges birding and hiking trips. Tourists can walk the well-maintained trails that lead to a coffee plantation and along the San Juan river to cascades and mineral springs. Boats can also be rented on the lake, and there's a zip-line canopy tour.

2 Cayo Levisa

Ringed by white-sand beaches, this tiny island (see p54) off the north coast has a resort hotel and can be reached by ferry from the mainland. A nearby coral reef has splendid crystal-clear dive sites, while the deeper waters farther offshore are populated with marlin and other game-fish. The mangroves are also a habitat for waterbirds (see p53).

3 Soroa

MAP C2 ■ Hotel & Villas Soroa: (48) 52 3534

Surrounded by forested mountains, Soroa, once a center for coffee prod-uction, is currently a holiday village offering a scenic escape for nature lovers. Attractions include a stunning orchid garden (see p16) displaying more than 700 species. A trail heads sharply downhill to the Cascadas El Salto waterfall, while more challeng-ing hikes lead to the Mirador de Venus – a mountaintop lookout with superlative views. The Hotel & Villas Soroa is a simple but delightful retreat.

Cascadas El Salto waterfall

4 Viñales

MAP B2 ■ **Casa de Don Tomás:** Calle Salvador Cisneros 140; (48) 79 6300 ■ **Casa de la Cultura:** Calle José Martí 5; (48) 77 8128; adm ■ **Centro de Visitantes:** 1 mile (1.6 km) SW of Viñales; (48) 79 6144; open 8am–8pm daily

The agricultural community of Viñales has preserved the colonial architecture of this tiny village. The main street is lined with red-tile-roofed cottages fronted by columned arcades. The Casa de Don Tomás, a replica of the 1822 building destroyed in 2008 by a hurricane, is now a restaurant. A church stands over Parque Martí, where the Casa de la Cultura hosts cultural activities. A visitor center sits atop a *mogote* nearby *(see p17)*.

5 Pinar del Río

MAP B3 ■ **Fábrica de Tabacos Francisco Donatién:** (48) 77 3069; open 9am–noon & 1–4pm Mon–Fri; adm

Founded in 1669, this is a peaceful town with a sloping main street lined with eclectic buildings, many with Art Nouveau facades. The Palacio de Guasch stands out for its flamboyant exterior. The town is a center of tobacco processing and is home to the Fábrica de Tabacos Francisco Donatién, the local cigar factory.

6 Vuelta Abajo

MAP B3 ■ **Finca El Pinar San Luís, Vegas Robaina** ■ (48) 79 7470 ■ **Open** 9am–5pm Mon–Sat ■ **Adm for guided tours**

To the west of the provincial capital, these fertile plains centered on the town of San Juan y Martínez are famed for their tobacco. The leaves, protected from the sun by fine netting, are cured in traditional

Viñales church

ranches. The Finca El Pinar Vegas Robaina, a private tobacco *finca* (ranch) owned by renowned farmer Alejandro Robaina, is worth a visit.

7 Parque Nacional Península de Guanahacabibes

MAP A3 ■ (48) 75 0366 ■ **Adm** ■ www.ecovida.cu

Occupying a slender peninsula jutting into the Gulf of Mexico at the western tip of Cuba *(see p50)*, this park – a UNESCO Biosphere Reserve – protects a rare dry forest habitat. Endangered mammals such as the endemic *jutía* and solenodon exist here, as do deer, wild pigs, iguanas, and more than 170 bird species. Guided hikes are offered from the Ecological Station. A sandy track runs to Cabo San Antonio, marked by a lighthouse built in 1849.

8 Cayo Largo

MAP F4

Lined with white-sand beaches, Cayo Largo offers horseback riding, sailing, and scuba diving. Excursions whisk you off to nearby isles that are home to flamingos and iguanas. Accommodations range from a fishing lodge to 4-star all-inclusives *(see p127)*. The island is popular for excursions from Havana and Varadero and for nude sunbathing.

Beachside resort at Cayo Largo

9 Nueva Gerona

MAP D4 ■ Iglesia Nuestra
Señora de los Dolores: (46) 32 3791;
hours vary ■ Museo de Historia
Natural: (46) 32 3143; open 8am–5pm
Tue–Sat, 8am–noon Sun; adm

The sleepy capital city of Isla de la
Juventud has a graceful colonial core
of venerable one-story buildings with
columns supporting red-tiled roofs.
The Iglesia Nuestra Señora de los
Dolores is a lovely church on the
main plaza, with a small museum.
The Museo de Historia Natural shows
re-creations of local natural habitats.

The derelict Presidio Modelo

10 Presidio Modelo

MAP D4 ■ (46) 32 5112 ■ Open
8am–4pm Tue–Sat, 8am–noon Sun
■ Adm (extra charge for cameras)

This former penitentiary (see p38) on
the outskirts of Nueva Gerona was
built in 1926. In October 1953, Fidel
Castro and 25 other revolutionaries
were imprisoned here after the failed
attack on the Moncada barracks (see
p37). Today the prison hospital is a
museum recalling the 20 months
they spent here. Castro's room still
contains the collection of books he
used to instruct fellow prisoners.

CORK PALM

Found only in a few tiny pockets
of the Sierra del Rosario, Cuba's
endemic *Palma corcho* is a primitive
member of the cycad family. Growing
in an ecosystem badly threatened by
deforestation, the species reproduces
with difficulty, although individual
palms live to be more than 300 years.
As a result, this so-called "living fossil"
faces possible extinction.

NORTH COAST DRIVE

> ### MORNING

Leave Havana in a rental car
and head west along Avenue
5ta, which leads past the **Latin
American School for Medical
Sciences**, where international
students receive free medical
training. Pass through the port
town of **Mariel**, onto Carretera
2-1-3, a winding and gently
rolling road frequented by
ox-drawn carts. After about two
hours of driving past sugarcane
fields, turn south at the sign for
Soroa (see p85) and follow the
road as it curls uphill through
pine forest. Take the time to
explore the orchid garden
and hike the short trail to the
Cascadas El Salto waterfall.
Enjoy lunch at one of the restaurants in the area before you go.

AFTERNOON

Returning to the highway, continue west through the towns
of **Bahía Honda** and **Las Pozas**,
with the Sierra del Rosario
mountains to the south. The **Pan
de Guajaibón** – a dramatic *mogote*
– can be reached by turning south
at the hamlet of Rancho Canelo.
Farther west beyond Las Pozas,
turn north for the ferry dock
to **Cayo Levisa** (see p85), where
you can enjoy an overnight stay
at a charming hotel. Boats depart
at 10am and 6pm. Alternatively,
continue west beyond **La Palma**
to **Viñales**. The road cuts through
tobacco fields before emerging
in the Valle de San Vicente. Turn
southward at the T-junction for
Viñales. Two affordable hotels
sit atop *mogotes* and *casas
particulares* (private rooms)
are also available.

See map on pp84–5

The Best of the Rest

① San Antonio de los Baños
MAP C2

This small colonial town has a museum of humor and echoes with laughter during its biennial Humorismo Gráfico festival.

María la Gorda

② María la Gorda
MAP A4

This remote and popular dive spot at the far west end of Cuba is set on a gorgeous bay full of coral and other marine life.

③ Cueva de los Portales

A dramatic cavern full of dripstone formations (see p17), which Che Guevara made his headquarters during the Cuban Missile Crisis.

④ Cuevas de Puntas del Este
MAP D4 ■ c/o Ecotur: Calle 24 & 31, Nueva Gerona; (46) 32 7101

A permit is required to visit these protected caves adorned with ancient Taíno pictographs.

⑤ Museo Finca El Abra
MAP D4 ■ Carretera Siguanea, km 2 ■ Open 9am–5pm Tue–Sat, 9am–1pm Sun ■ Adm

This simple colonial-era farm, where José Martí stayed during his house arrest in 1870, is now a museum.

⑥ Playa Jibacoa
MAP E2

Jibacoa is a series of beaches popular with Cuban families. Accommodations range from all-inclusive resorts to simple camps popular with Cubans.

⑦ Criadero de Cocodrilos
MAP D4 ■ c/o Ecotur: Calle 24 & 31, Nueva Gerona; (46) 32 7101; ecoturij@enet.cu; guide compulsory

Cuba's endemic crocodile is raised here for reintroduction into the wild. Visit in the early morning to witness feeding time.

⑧ Reserva Ecológico Los Indios
MAP C4 ■ c/o Ecotur: Calle 24 & 31, Nueva Gerona; (46) 32 7101; eco turij@enet.cu; guide compulsory

These mangroves, grasslands, and forests on the southwest shores of Isla de la Juventud teem with life.

⑨ Gran Caverna de Santo Tomás
MAP B2 ■ 20 miles (32 km) west of Viñales ■ (48) 68 1214 ■ Guided tours

In the heart of a *mogote*-studded valley, the Gran Caverna de Santo Tomás (see p16) form the largest underground system in Cuba.

Gran Caverna de Santo Tomás

⑩ Parque Nacional Punta Francés
MAP C4

At the southwest tip of Isla de la Juventud, stunning coral formations and numerous wrecks make this a superb spot for diving.

Outdoor Activities

Climbing a steep limestone cliff, or mogote, in the Valle de Viñales

 Hiking
Las Terrazas and Soroa (see p16) are perfect places for walking, from short strolls to challenging hikes. The two hotels located here can arrange guides (see p130).

2 **Horseback Riding**
 Cubanacán: Calle Salvador Cisneros 63c ▪ (48) 79 6393
Head for the Mural de la Prehistoria at Valle de Viñales (see p17), or ask at the Cubanacán office in the village.

3 **Caving**
Sociedad Espeleológica: 7209 2885 ▪ Centro de Visitantes: (48) 68 1214
Gran Caverna de Santo Tomás is the place to go to explore Cuba's hidden depths. The Sociedad Espeleológica can arrange visits for serious cavers.

4 **Diving**
Acclaimed for the finest diving in Cuba, La Costa de los Piratas (Pirate Coast) off Punta Francés offers dozens of fantastic dive sites – including the opportunity to explore the wrecks of several sunken Spanish galleons.

5 **Cycling**
 The dramatic scenery and peaceful, paved roads of the Valle de Viñales (see p50) guarantee cyclists an experience to remember.

6 **Rock-Climbing**
Scaling the mogotes of the Valle de Viñales requires skill; more than 100 established climbs have been pioneered by local enthusiasts.

7 **Bird-Watching**
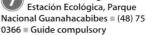 Estación Ecológica, Parque Nacional Guanahacabibes ▪ (48) 75 0366 ▪ Guide compulsory
The Guanahacabibes Peninsula is home to more than 170 bird species, including a number of endemics best seen on guided hikes through the La Bajada preserve.

8 **Swimming**
Cayo Levisa ▪ (48) 75 6501
The crystal-clear waters surrounding Cayo Levisa are ideal for swimming and snorkeling, and the lakes at Las Terrazas (see p16) are great for refreshing dips.

9 **Wildlife Viewing**
View various types of fauna including flamingos, iguanas, and monkeys that inhabit the remote cays west of Cayo Largo, from where excursions are offered.

10 **Fishing**
The waters off Cayo Largo offer anglers plenty of thrills, from tiny but challenging bone-fish to marlin, which put up a rod-bending struggle to escape.

See map on pp84–5 ←

Wildlife

Mangroves

Growing at the boundary of land and sea, mangroves form a tangled web of interlocking roots that rise from the waters and provide shelter for juvenile marine creatures. Five species grow in Cuba along both Caribbean and Atlantic shores.

2 Whale Sharks

Scuba divers often have close encounters with whale sharks in the warm waters of the Bahía de Corrientes and off Punta Francés.

3 Turtles

Female marine turtles crawl onto the shores of pristine Cuban beaches to lay their eggs above the high-water mark. A farm on Cayo Largo specializes in breeding green and hawksbill turtles.

4 Bone-fish

This silvery fish is well-camouflaged against the sandy bottoms of shallow lagoons and is notorious for the challenging fight it gives anglers. Cayo Largo is a prime site for bone-fishing.

5 Spoonbills

This handsome, rose-colored wading bird has a spatulate bill and is a member of the Ibis family. It nests in among the mangroves and can be seen in the Refugio Ecológico Los Indios (see p88).

Crocodiles

The swamplands of southern Isla de la Juventud harbor a large population of Cuban crocodiles (see p52). A successful breeding program has brought the species back from the edge of extinction.

7 Parrots

Cuba's endemic parrot (see p52) is easily recognized, with its noisy mating calls, red cheeks, white forehead, and blue wing-tips. The dry tropical forests of the Isla de la Juventud have the largest parrot population in Cuba.

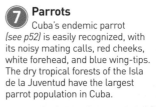
Cuban amazon parrots

8 Marlin
MAP A4 ■ María la Gorda: (48) 75 0118

The fast-flowing Gulf Stream off the north coast of Pinar del Río is a veritable highway for marlin, which give sport-fishers a tremendous fight. María la Gorda has a marina and offers sport-fishing charters.

9 Iguanas

Looking almost lifeless, these giant herbivorous lizards (see p52) crawl around the arid terrain of the Península de Guanahacabibes (see p50) and the infertile Archipiélago de los Canarreos.

Manatees

These endangered marine mammals inhabit the coastal lagoons off both north and south shores and, although rarely seen, are very common off the Golfo de Guanahacabibes. Manatees feed on seabed grasses and other vegetation.

Cuban crocodile

Restaurants

PRICE CATEGORIES

For a three-course meal with half a bottle of wine (or equivalent meal), taxes, and extra charges

$ under CUC$15 $$ CUC$15–25 $$$ over CUC$25

 La Fonda de Mercedes
MAP C2 ■ Complejo Las Terrazas ■ c/o (48) 57 8555 ■ $$

This *paladar* (private restaurant) serves traditional Cuban meals on a terrace overlooking a lake.

2 Casa del Campesino
MAP C2 ■ Complejo Las Terrazas ■ c/o (48) 57 8555 ■ $

A farmstead where traditional Cuban dishes are prepared in an outdoor oven and enjoyed under a thatched roof. Popular with tour groups.

3 Restaurante Rumayor
MAP B3 ■ Av. a Viñales, Pinar del Río town ■ (48) 76 3007 ■ $$

The *comida criollo* (cuban fare) here is average, but this thatched restaurant is worth a visit for its Tiki-style decor, African drums, and cabaret.

4 Eco-Restaurante El Romero
MAP C2 ■ Complejo Las Terrazas ■ c/o (48) 57 8555 ■ $

Chef Tito presides over a vegetarian paradise, serving delicious and original dishes and juices.

5 Restaurante Las Arcadas
MAP B2 ■ Rancho San Vicente, Carretera a Puerto Esperanza, km 33 ■ (48) 79 6201 ■ $$

This hotel restaurant overlooks lush grounds. It serves seafood, pasta, and Cuban staples.

 Casa de Don Tomás
MAP B2 ■ Calle Salvador Cisneros 147, Viñales ■ (48) 79 6300 ■ $$

Housed in a reconstructed historic building, Casa de Don Tomás specializes in *delicias de Don Tomás*, a pork, chicken, and lobster dish, served with rice, beans, and *tostones* (fried plantains). There is traditional live music.

7 Casa del Veguero
MAP B2 ■ Carretera de Viñales, km 23 ■ (48) 79 6080 ■ $$

Set amid tobacco fields, this thatched open-air restaurant serves prix-fixe *criollo* meals and includes tours of the tobacco farm. Musicians play while you eat.

8 Restaurante Vera
MAP B2 ■ Hotel Los Jazmines, Carretera de Viñales, km 23 ■ (48) 79 6205 ■ $$

Overlooking the Valle de Viñales from atop a *mogote* (see p17), this location offers the most dramatic view of any restaurant in Cuba.

Lobster at El Balcón de las Tecas

9 El Balcón de las Tecas
MAP C2 ■ Hotel La Moka, Las Terrazas ■ (48) 57 8602 ■ $$

This is an elegant place to enjoy lobster dishes and specialties such as delicious roast chicken.

 El Olivo
MAP B2 ■ Calle Salvador Cisneros 89, Viñales ■ (48) 69 6654 ■ $$

This private restaurant on the main street of Viñales delivers mouth-watering Italian and Spanish dishes, plus local specials.

See map on pp84–5

🔟 Central Cuba West

Encompassing the provinces of Matanzas, Cienfuegos, and Santa Clara, Central Cuba West is the island's traditional center of tourism. Visitors flock to the white sands of Varadero, and farther east, the Cayos de Villa Clara are fast developing into booming tourist spots. The region is also blessed with wilderness – the Zapata Peninsula shelters Cuban crocodiles and birdlife, while the pine-clad Sierra del Escambray offers mountain trails and waterfalls. History fans are drawn to museums at Playa Girón and Santa Clara. Cienfuegos

is blessed with many imposing colonial structures and fin-de-siècle mansions, while Matanzas thrums to the rhythms of Afro-Cuban music and dance. At Christmas, the sleepy town of Remedios comes alive with fireworks fever.

Iglesia Virgen del Buen Viaje, Remedios

AREA MAP OF CENTRAL CUBA WEST

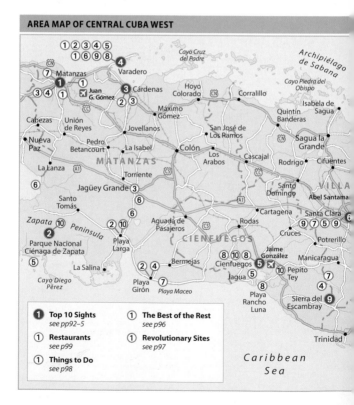

1 Top 10 Sights
see pp92–5

① Restaurants
see p99

① Things to Do
see p98

① The Best of the Rest
see p96

① Revolutionary Sites
see p97

San Severino Castle, Matanzas

1 Matanzas

MAP E2 ■ Museo Farmacéutico: Plaza de la Libertad; (45) 24 3179; open 10am–5pm daily; adm ■ Castillo de San Severino: Zona Industrial; (45) 28 3259; open 9am–4pm Mon–Sat, 9am–noon Sun; adm

This historic port town, which evolved as a trading center for sugar and slaves, was dubbed the "Athens of Cuba" when artistic life flourished here during the 19th century. Plaza de la Libertad and Plaza de la Vigía are home to the Catedral de San Carlos and Museo Farmacéutico. Visit San Severino castle's slave-trade museum and, outside town, Cuevas de Bellamar's caverns.

2 Parque Nacional Ciénaga de Zapata

MAP E3 ■ National Park Office: Playa Larga; (45) 98 7249; open 8am–4:30pm daily; adm includes a guide

This vast park is Cuba's most complete wildlife preserve. Swampland smothers the region, while mangroves, reeds, and wet forests also provide varied habitats that support more than 200 bird species, such as the Cuban pygmy owl and the tiny *zunzuncito (see p53)*. Manatees swim in coastal lagoons, where Cuban crocodiles also lurk, and flamingos flock to Laguna de las Salinas. Official guides lead nature-oriented tours, and most local inhabitants now make a living by renting rooms or acting as guides for tourists.

Museo Oscar María de Rojas, Cardenas

3 Cárdenas
MAP F2

The rather run-down port town of Cárdenas offers some intriguing attractions. A good starting point is tiny Parque Colón, where a statue of Christopher Columbus stands in front of the 1826 Catedral de la Concepción Inmaculada. The Museo Oscar María de Rojas *(see p46)* has fascinating displays with some artifacts dating back to pre-Columbian days. Horse-drawn taxi-cabs traverse town.

Atlantic
Ocean

Cayos
del Pajonal

Cayos de
Villa Clara
7

rucijada   **9**

ARA   **10** Caibarién   *Bahía de*
8   *Buena Vista*
Remedios

                              Jaguajay

acetas
              Jarahueca   Mayajigua

            Cabaiguán   San Felipe

SANCTI
SPÍRITUS   Jatibonico
        Sancti
        Spíritus   Majagua

        Banao
                La Ferrolana Limones
edro   La Unión   Palmero

    Playa
ayabacoa   0 kilometers   30
                0 miles   30

Luxury hotels line the beach at Varadero

④ Varadero
MAP F2

The beach here, at Cuba's top resort, offers plenty of watersports, but shade is in short supply. Away from the beach, regional attractions include hiking and scuba diving. Golfers are also catered for at the 18-hole course at Mansión Xanadú *(see p131)*. Most hotels in the area are large, all-inclusive resorts, but visitors can also choose from a handful of smaller options.

Palacio del Valle, Cienfuegos

⑤ Cienfuegos
MAP G3

Set on the shores of a bay, Cienfuegos was founded in 1819, when French settlers laid out a grid around the Plaza de Armas, now Plaza Martí. The Paseo del Prado slopes down to the Punta Gorda district, where Art Nouveau and mid-20th-century Modernist homes can be rented. A highlight of any visit is a meal at Palacio del Valle, a mansion decorated in Moorish fashion *(see p99)*.

⑥ Santa Clara
MAP H3 ■ Teatro de la Caridad, Parque Vidal 3; (45) 20 5548; open 9am–4pm Mon–Sat; adm

Known as the "city of the heroic guerrilla," Santa Clara is an industrial and university town from where, in 1958, Che Guevara led the final battle to topple Batista *(see p37)*. Visitors flock to sites associated with the battle, such as the Tren Blindado (a derailed armored train) and the Complejo Escultórico Ernesto Che Guevara *(see p97)*. Also of interest is the frescoed ceiling of the Teatro de la Caridad (Charity Theater).

⑦ Cayos de Villa Clara
MAP J1

These islands lie 45 miles (72 km) from the mainland, to which they are connected by a very narrow *pedraplén* (causeway). The calm peacock-blue sea is protected by a coral reef and is ideal for swimming and snorkeling – the deeper waters beyond the reef offer diving. Catamaran and sport-fishing excursions depart from a marina.

> **MANJUARÍ**
>
> This primitive fish from the antediluvian dawn evolved at least 270 million years ago, about the time the first reptiles crawled out of the seas. Growing to 6 ft (2 m) long, it has an elongated snout like a crocodile's. Its scaly skin is covered with natural oil. Endemic to Cuba, the dark green fish inhabits the Zapata swamps.

8 Remedios

MAP H3 ■ Museo de la Música Alejandro García Caturla: (42) 39 6851; open 9am–noon, 1–5pm Tue–Sat, 9am–noon Sun; adm ■ Museo de las Parrandas: open 9am–noon, 1–6pm Tue–Sat, 9am–1pm Sun; adm

Founded in 1578, this is one of Cuba's most charming colonial cities. The Museo de la Música Alejandro García Caturla displays musical instruments, while the Museo de las Parrandas exhibits objects linked to the city's famous Christmas festival (see p69).

Colonnaded buildings in Remedios

9 Sierra del Escambray

MAP H3

Spanning three provinces, this rugged mountain range rises inland from the Caribbean coast, reaching 3,790 ft (1,155 m) atop Pico San Juan. Coffee is farmed on the lower slopes, while the densely forested upper slopes are of great ecological value for their plants and profuse birdlife. Topes de Collantes (see p51) offers accommodation and is a base for guided nature hikes.

10 Caibarién

MAP H3

A once-important port town that still lives partly off its humble fishing fleet, sprawling Caibarién has a dishevelled countenance and awaits a renaissance of its incredible wealth of architecture, with buildings from Neo-Classical to Art Nouveau centered on Parque de la Libertad. The town also has beaches, and mangroves teeming with birds.

JAGÜEY GRANDE TO CIENFUEGOS DRIVE

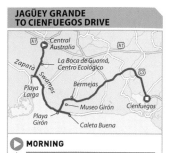

▶ MORNING

Start your day early with a visit to **Central Australia** (see p19). After a brief tour, including a possible steam-train ride, drive south along the ruler-straight road with the grassy swamps of **Zapata** (see pp18–19) on each side. Stop off at **La Boca de Guamá** to see the crocodiles and then at **Centro Ecológico**, where an ecological trail lets you experience the Zapata ecosystems first-hand. At **Playa Larga**, follow the main road south along the shoreline toward **Playa Girón**. Take time to browse the Bay of Pigs exhibits and displays (see p37) at the fascinating **Museo Girón** (see p19) then continue 5 miles (8 km) east to **Caleta Buena** (see p19). Enjoy lunch and an hour or two snorkeling in this sheltered cove. Note that in March and April, the road is smothered with crabs migrating inland to spawn. They are a hazard; ensure that your tires have plenty of tread to reduce the chance of getting a puncture from broken shells.

AFTERNOON

Retrace your path to Playa Girón and turn north; the route is potholed in places. At **Bermejas**, turn right. Observe daily rural Cuban life in the remote settlements you pass through. Turn right onto Carretera 3-1-2, the main highway that leads to the well-planned maritime city of **Cienfuegos**. Spend the rest of the day admiring its Neo-Classical structures, ending with a seafood meal at the exotic **Palacio del Valle** (see p99).

See map on pp92–3 ←

The Best of the Rest

① Cuevas de Bellamar
MAP E2 ▪ Carretera de las Cuevas de Bellamar ▪ (45) 25 3538 ▪ Open 9:30am–5pm Tue–Sun ▪ Adm ▪ Seven tours daily

These extensive caves have fascinating dripstone features. A small museum located here details the geological processes.

② Museo Girón
This museum, replete with gory photographs and bloody uniforms, recalls the Bay of Pigs invasion (see p19). Displays include a Sea Fury plane.

③ Fiesta Finca Campesina
MAP F3 ▪ Autopista Nacional, km 142, Jagüey Grande ▪ (45) 91 2045 ▪ Open 9am–5pm ▪ Adm

This re-creation of a typical Cuban farm has a zoo with crocodiles, a sugarcane press, and buffalo rides.

④ El Nicho
MAP G3 ▪ 28 miles (45 km) northwest of Trinidad ▪ (43) 43 3351 ▪ Adm

Cuba's most beautiful waterfall plummets down the north side of the Sierra Escambray into cool, turquoise pools.

Cannons at Castillo de Jagua

⑤ Castillo de Jagua
MAP G3 ▪ Poblado Castillo de Jagua ▪ (43) 59 6402 ▪ Open 9am–5pm Mon–Sat, 9am–1pm Sun ▪ Adm

This tiny fortress guarding the entrance to Cienfuegos Bay still has a working drawbridge across the moat.

The lagoon at Boca de Guamá

⑥ Boca de Guamá
MAP F3 ▪ (45) 91 5662 ▪ Adm

Beside Laguna del Tesoro, this tourist facility has a crocodile farm and offers boat tours of the lagoon.

⑦ Lago Hanabanilla
MAP H3 ▪ Hotel Hanabanilla: (42) 20 8461

This reservoir is on the Sierra del Escambray's northern slopes. The no-frills Hotel Hanabanilla stands over the western shore.

⑧ Playa Rancho Luna
MAP G3 ▪ Faro Luna Dive Center: (43) 54 8040 ▪ Delfinario: (43) 54 8120 ▪ 8:30am–4:30pm Thu–Tue ▪ Adm (extra to swim with dolphins)

This attractive beach has two tourist hotels, the Faro Luna Dive Center, and a dolphinarium, where dolphins and sea lions perform.

⑨ Museo de Agroindustria Azucarero Marcelo Salado
MAP H3 ▪ (42) 36 3286 ▪ Open 9am–4:30pm Mon–Fri, alternate Sat ▪ Adm

Learn about the history of Cuba's sugar industry and hop aboard for a ride on one of this museum's antique steam trains.

⑩ Jardín Botánico Soledad
MAP G3 ▪ Pepito Tey ▪ (43) 54 5115 ▪ Open 8am–5pm ▪ Adm

A botanical garden houses one of the world's largest palm collections, as well as other exotic plants.

See map on pp92–3

Revolutionary Sites

1 **Castillo El Morrillo**
MAP F2 ▪ Canímar
▪ Open 9am–4pm Tue–Sun

This fortress houses the mausoleum of two martyred revolutionary leaders: Antonio Guiteras Holmes and Carlos Aponte Hernández.

2 **Museo de la Batalla de Ideas**
MAP F2 ▪ Av. 6 between 11 & 12, Cárdenas: (45) 52 7599 ▪ Open 9am–5pm Tue–Sat, 9am–1pm Sun ▪ Adm

A museum recounts the custody battle over Elián González, a Cuban boy rescued from sea off Miami.

3 **Museo Casa Natal de José Antonio Echeverría**
MAP F2 ▪ Genes between Calzada & Coronel Verdugo, Cárdenas ▪ (45) 52 4145 ▪ Open 9am–6pm Tue–Sat, 9am–1pm Sun ▪ Adm

This museum was once the home of José Antonio Echeverría (see p41).

4 **Museo Girón**
The Cuban version of the Bay of Pigs invasion is recounted at this museum (see p19).

5 **Tren Blindado**
MAP H3 ▪ Av. Independencia btwn Línea & Puente de la Cruz, Santa Clara ▪ (42) 20 2758 ▪ Open 9am–5pm Mon–Sat ▪ Adm

This monument re-creates the derailing of an armored train by Che's guerrillas using the original carriages.

6 **Central Australia**
This site preserves the building that was Castro's headquarters during the Bay of Pigs (see p19).

7 **Complejo Escultórico Ernesto Che Guevara**
MAP H3 ▪ Plaza de la Revolución, Santa Clara ▪ (42) 20 5878 ▪ Open 9am–4pm Tue–Sun

A statue of Che looms over this site, which features the mausoleum where his body is interred (see p39).

8 **Museo Naval**
MAP G3 ▪ Calle 21 & Av. 62, Cienfuegos ▪ (43) 51 9143 ▪ Open 10am–6pm Tue–Sat, 9am–1pm Sun ▪ Adm

The headquarters of an anti-Batista revolt on September 5, 1957, this is now a naval museum.

9 **Museo Provincial Abel Santamaría**
MAP H3 ▪ Calle Esquerra ▪ (42) 20 3041 ▪ Open 8:30am–4:30pm Mon–Fri, 9am–1pm Sun ▪ Adm

A museum dedicated to the revolutionary movement in Santa Clara is housed in this former military barracks.

10 **Playa Larga**
MAP F3
On April 17, 1961, CIA-sponsored Cuban exiles landed on this beach (see p37).

Tren Blindado

Things to Do

Boats off the beach at Varadero

1 Sailing

Small sailing boats can be rented at Rancho Luna and Varadero (see p94), from where boat trips to outlying cays depart and tropical cocktails are served as the sun sets.

2 Scuba Diving

Diving enthusiasts will enjoy the region's north and south shores. Playa Larga (see p97) is famed for its coral reefs, and Varadero is popular for its sunken warships.

3 Learning to Dance

Matanzas (see p93) is an excellent venue for learning to dance like a Cuban. Festivals that take place in October and November feature dance workshops.

4 Riding the Hershey Train

Connecting Matanzas to Casablanca, Havana, this commuter train passes through sugarcane fields once owned by the Hershey chocolate factory.

5 Angling for Bone-Fish

The region offers some of the best bone-fishing in the Caribbean. The shallow lagoons off southern Zapata (see p93) and Cayos de Villa Clara (see p94) are the best spots. Hotels offer guided fishing trips.

6 Horse-Carriage Tour

Formal excursions by colonial-era, horse-drawn carriages are a great way to explore Varadero and Cienfuegos (see p94), while in all other cities you can hop aboard one of the rickety *coches* that ply the main streets as slow-moving taxis for locals.

7 Snorkeling at Caleta Buena

MAP F3

The whole region is very good for snorkeling, but this cove (see p19) near Playa Girón offers a display of corals, sponges, and tropical fish. Snorkeling gear is available for rent. Lunch and snacks are served during the course of the day.

8 Paragliding

Varadero is the place for this thrilling activity, where you strap on a harness attached to a giant kite pulled by a speedboat. In seconds you're soaring, with a bird's-eye view of the beach resort far below.

9 Golf

MAP F2 ■ Av. Las Américas, km 8.5 ■ (45) 66 7788 ■ www.varaderogolfclub.com

The Varadero Golf Club, at Mansion Xanadú, is Cuba's only 18-hole golf course, although more are planned. Laid out along the shore, it offers a demanding breeze-swept challenge between the sands and a lagoon.

Cuban emerald hummingbird

10 Birding

Parque National Ciénaga de Zapata and the Sierra del Escambray teem with exotic bird species. Look for parrots and hummingbirds, and flamingos in the lagoons (see p52).

Restaurants

PRICE CATEGORIES
For a three-course meal with half a bottle of wine (or equivalent meal), taxes and extra charges

$ under CUC$15 $$ CUC$15–25 $$$ over CUC$25

1 El Mesón del Quijote
MAP F2 ■ Av. Las Américas, Varadero ■ (45) 66 7796 ■ $$

Perched on top of a grassy hill, this restaurant re-creates the mood of a Spanish *bodega* with its rustic decor.

2 Varadero 60
MAP F2 ■ Av. 60 & Calle 60, Varadero ■ (45) 61 3986 ■ $

Housed in a converted mansion, this restaurant sporting 1950s decor serves wood-fired dishes such as shrimp with brandy.

3 Salsa Suárez
MAP F2 ■ Calle 31 103, Varadero ■ (45) 61 2009 ■ $$

This classy, private restaurant has a charming and sophisticated nautical-themed dining room. Try the seafood cannelloni.

4 Kike-Kcho
MAP F1 ■ Autopista Sur y Final, Varadero ■ (45) 66 4115 ■ $$

Standing on stilts over the Bahía de Cárdenas, this upscale seafood restaurant is one of Varadero's most sophisticated, and is decorated with works by the Cuban artist Kcho.

5 Restaurante La Fondue
MAP F2 ■ Av. 1ra & Calle 62, Varadero ■ (45) 66 7747 ■ $$

Imported cheeses find their way into creative fondues, but squid in tomato sauce is also on the menu.

6 Restaurante Colibrí
MAP F3 ■ Boca de Guamá ■ (45) 91 5662 ■ Closed for dinner ■ $$

A pleasant restaurant on the road to Zapata and Playa Larga. Crocodile dishes are a specialty.

7 Paladar la Mallorca
MAP E2 ■ Calle 334 7335, Matanzas ■ (45) 28 3281 ■ $

The hilltop setting makes this private restaurant hard to find but its *criolla* cuisine is suitably rewarding.

8 Palacio del Valle
MAP G3 ■ Calle 37 & Av. 0, Cienfuegos ■ (43) 55 1003 ■ $$

The fare may be average, but the surroundings astound in this grandiose mansion in Mughal style, with spectacular views of the bay. The terrace is perfect for sipping a cocktail while enjoying the sunset. Musicians entertain in the evenings.

The lavish interior of Palacio del Valle

9 Paladar Hostal Florida Center
MAP H3 ■ Calle Maestra Nicolasa 56, Santa Clara ■ (42) 20 8161 ■ $

Dine on the flower-filled patio of this beautiful 19th-century colonial home. Host Angel cooks and serves delicious food, such as shrimp in tomato sauce, to the accompaniment of Cuban tunes.

10 Finca del Mar
MAP G3 ■ Calle 35 between 18 & 20, Cienfuegos ■ (43) 52 6598 ■ $$

This class act is the best private restaurant in town. Owner Omar is in charge of delicious *nouvelle* and traditional dishes. There is also a delightful outdoor dining terrace with sea views.

See map on pp92 3 ←

TOP 10 Central Cuba East

From the atmospheric colonial city of Trinidad to the gorgeous beaches of the Jardines del Rey, this region is one of the most exciting in Cuba. The terrain ranges from the sugar territory of the Valle de los Ingenios and the forested mountains around Topes de Collantes to the tourist-friendly white-sand spots in Cayo Coco and Cayo Guillermo. Trinidad, one of Cuba's most vibrant historic cities, is a wonderful base for exploring Topes and for scuba diving off the beach at nearby Playa Ancón. Camagüey is noted for its colonial architecture. The Carretera Central connects the key sites, but the pristine maritime wilderness of Jardines de la Reina is accessible solely by boat.

Iznaga Tower, Trinidad

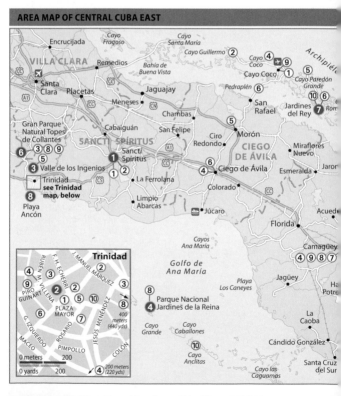

AREA MAP OF CENTRAL CUBA EAST

Previous pages Rock formations at Gran Parque Natural Topes de Collantes

Musicians in Sancti Spíritus

1 Sancti Spíritus
MAP J3 ■ Iglesia Parroquial
Mayor del Espíritu Santo: Calle
Agramonte Oeste 58, (41) 32
4855; adm

Founded in 1522, this city is often
overlooked by visitors, who tend
to focus on neighboring Trinidad.
The historic core of Sancti Spíritus
has elegant mansions and brightly
colored colonial homes graced by
wrought-iron lanterns and grills.
Sights include the Yayabo bridge
and Parque Serafín Sánchez. The
highlight is Plaza Honorato, with
its Casa de la Trova and the lovely
Iglesia Parroquial Mayor del Espíritu
Santo – a 17th-century church with
a spectacular ceiling.

2 Trinidad
Cuba's most endearing
colonial city was founded in 1514
by Diego Velázquez and named
a UNESCO World Heritage Site in
1988. Closed to traffic, the cobbled
streets have remained largely
unchanged since the 18th century,
when Trinidad grew wealthy from
trade in slavery and sugar. The
museums, churches, and plazas
are intriguing, but the real joy is in
wandering the narrow streets and
observing daily life (see pp20–21).

Valle de los Ingenios

3 Valle de los Ingenios
MAP H4 ■ Hacienda Manaca
Iznaga: Iznaga; (41) 99 7241; adm

A broad carpet of sugarcane covers
this fertile vale northeast of Trinidad.
The area gets its name from the
many *ingenios* (sugar mills) built
during the 18th and 19th centuries,
when vast sugar plantations
occupied the entire valley. While
many of the sugarcane estates are
in the process of being restored as
museums, the main house of the
Hacienda Manaca Iznaga estate has
been converted into a restaurant.
Climb its 147-ft (45-m) tower for
a great view of the valley.

Parque Nacional Jardines de la Reina

(4) Parque Nacional Jardines de la Reina

MAP J4 ■ Avalon Dive Center; www.cubandivingcenters.com

Over 600 deserted isles scattered off the Ciego de Ávila and Camagüey provinces form an oceanic Eden protected by a long coral reef. Marine turtles lay their eggs on beaches, while iguanas laze in the sun and flamingos wade in the shallows. Four cruise vessels and a floating hotel cater to anglers and divers. The Avalon Dive Center at Júcaro handles all visiting arrangements.

(5) Camagüey

The plazas of Cuba's third-largest city are lined with colonial and Neo-Classical buildings. The city's network of streets – designed to thwart pirates – can be confusing to visitors. Sites include the Catedral, museums, and the Teatro Principal – home to the Ballet de Camagüey. The best of the city's nightlife can be experienced at the Casa de la Trova on Plaza Agramonte *(see pp26–7)*.

(6) Gran Parque Natural Topes de Collantes

MAP H4 ■ Gaviota Topes de Collantes: (42) 54 0117 ■ Gaviota Trinidad: (41) 99 6235

The steep drive to the northwest of Trinidad is well rewarded at Topes de Collantes, which functions as a base for hikes to the El Nicho waterfall and the colonial-era coffee estate at Finca Codina, where caves and a beautiful orchid garden can be explored. Topes has some hotels in its vicinity, plus a tourist information center, and the Gaviota, which oversees the complex, organizes tours and guides, including excursions from nearby Trinidad.

(7) Jardines del Rey

Off the north coast of Ciego de Ávila and Camagüey, the Jardines del Rey (King's Gardens) archipelago comprises about 400 islands, mostly uninhabited. Cayo Coco, one of the largest isles, and neighboring Cayo Guillermo have tourist hotels and watersports along their beaches. The diving is superb here, and flamingos flock to the inshore lagoons *(see pp24–5)*.

(8) Playa Ancón
MAP H4

The slender Península de Ancón south of Trinidad is lined by a fine, white-sand beach *(see p20)* served by three tourist hotels. With shallow waters good for swimming and

Camagüey's colorful city center

LA TROCHA

A line of defence was built by the Spanish during the 19th-century Wars of Independence to block the advance of Cuban nationalist forces, the *mambises*. La Trocha stretched across Cuba from Morón, north of Ciego de Ávila, to Júcaro, on the Caribbean coast, and featured fortified towers.

snorkeling, it is also frequented by the locals. A dive center arranges trips to Cayo Blanco to view the fabulous black coral formations. A marina rents out sailboats to visitors prior to their arrival in Cuba.

Secluded Playa Santa Lucía

⑨ Playa Santa Lucía
MAP M3

Proclaimed a beach-lovers' paradise by the Cuban tourist board, this isolated resort has a lovely beach and fantastic opportunities for diving and seeing bull sharks being hand fed. Horse-drawn carriages visit nearby Playa Los Cocos, an even lovelier beach adjoining a ramshackle fishing village. Dining and entertainment are limited to the all-inclusive hotels.

⑩ Las Tunas
MAP M4 ▪ Museo Histórico Provincial: Calle Francisco Varona and Colón; (31) 34 8201; open 9am–5pm Tue–Sat, 8am–noon Sun; adm

Located between central and eastern Cuba, Las Tunas suffered during the Wars of Independence (see p36), when it was razed by fire. Carretera Central, the national highway, runs through the heart of the city, and is lined with charming houses. The main square features a museum of provincial history, and the local tradition of ceramic art thrives here.

A DAY IN CAMAGÜEY

▶ **MORNING**

A day is barely enough to explore this historically significant town. Get an early start in the morning in **Parque Agramonte** (see p27) to see the equestrian statue, the cathedral, and **Casa de la Trova**. Exit the square by following Calle Cisneros south. After two blocks, turn right. The street brings you to **Plaza San Juan de Dios** (see p26), surrounded by 18th-century houses. Explore the museum inside the Iglesia y Hospital San Juan de Dios, then follow Calle Matias west three blocks. Turn right onto Calle 24 de Febrero. After five blocks, cobbled **Plaza del Carmen** (see p26) opens to the northwest at the junction with Calle Martí, and has life-like sculptures scattered about. Lunch on *bolice mechado* at **La Campaña de Toledo** (see p109).

AFTERNOON

Retrace your steps to Calle Martí and follow it east to Parque Agramonte. Turn left onto Calle Cisneros to reach **Plaza de los Trabajadores**. On your right, **Casa Natal Ignacio Agramonte** (see p26) is worth a peek before exploring the **Catedral Nuestra Señora de la Merced** (see p26). Don't miss its silver sepulchre. Exit the square to the northwest and walk one block to the **Teatro Principal** (see p27) on your right. Then head north along Calle Enrique José to the **Museo Ignacio Agramonte** (see p27). Continue south along Calle República to return to the center.

See map on pp102–3 ←

Colonial Trinidad

1 Plaza Mayor
Trinidad's main square is surrounded by 18th-century mansions. Two bronze greyhounds on the south side are popular with kids (see p20).

Convento de San Francisco de Asís

2 Convento de San Francisco de Asís
MAP Y1 ■ Calle Hernández Echerri 59 & Guinart ■ (41) 99 4121 ■ Open 9am–5pm daily ■ Adm
Built in 1730 by Franciscan monks, this convent is currently home to the Museo de la Lucha Contra Bandidos.

3 Palacio Brunet
Boasting marble floors, decorative tilework, and fan windows, this mansion is now the Museo Romántico, which features period furniture (see p20).

4 Plazuela de Jigüe
MAP Y1
This plaza was named after the jigüe (acacia) tree beneath which Father Bartolomé de las Casas celebrated the city's first mass in 1514.

5 Iglesia Parroquial de la Santísima Trinidad
MAP Z1 ■ Plaza Mayor
The Church of the Holy Trinity was built in 1892 on the site of the original parish church and has a Gothic altar.

6 Palacio Cantero
Home to the Museo Histórico, this gem is filled with sumptuous period furnishings and exhibits on Trinidad's history (see p21).

7 Museo de Arquitectura Colonial
This exquisite museum has excellent displays showing the evolution of architectural styles specific to Trinidad (see p46).

8 Iglesia de Santa Ana
MAP J3 ■ Calle Camilo Cienfuegos & Calle José Mendoza
At the northeast corner of the old city, this semi-derelict 18th-century church stands over a small plaza. There's also a lively cultural center located in a former prison.

9 Casa Templo de Santería Yemayá
MAP Y1 ■ Rubén Martínez Villena 59
Learn about the lores of Santería, the syncretic Afro-Cuban religion, at Casa Templo. This colonial home of a practitioner has an altar dedicated to Yemayá, the Virgin of Regla.

Casa de Don Rafael Ortíz

10 Casa de Don Rafael Ortíz
MAP Y1 ■ Calle Rubén Martínez Villena & Calle Bolívar ■ (41) 99 4432 ■ Open 8am–5pm Tue–Sat, 8am–1pm Sun–Mon
This early 19th-century mansion has an art gallery and a balcony with wonderful views of the plaza.

➤ See map on pp102–3

The Cays

1 Diving with Sharks

Certified divers can experience thrilling encounters with sharks on organized dives at Cayo Coco and Playa Santa Lucía. Whale sharks can be seen at Jardines de la Reina.

Scuba diver filming sharks

2 Cayo Guillermo

Linked to Cayo Coco by a narrow causeway, this small cay is blessed with stunning beaches and warm waters. Its bountiful mangroves provide good opportunities for those interested in bird-watching (see p24)

3 Cayo Sabinal

A remote cay that is accessible solely by a rough dirt road or by boat excursions from Playa Santa Lucía, Cayo Sabinal has three spectacular beaches, but facilities are scarce. Wild pigs roam the scrub-covered interior (see p25).

4 Cayo Coco
MAP K2

More than 14 miles (23 km) of gorgeous white beaches, crystal-clear turquoise ocean, and excellent all-inclusive hotels draw visitors from far and wide to Cayo Coco.

5 Cayo Paredón Grande
MAP L2

This scrub-covered cay offers a beach with a superb bar. Water sports can also be arranged through your hotel. Built in 1859, the intriguing Faro Diego Velázquez lighthouse, is located here.

Faro Diego Velázquez lighthouse

6 Pedraplén

This causeway connects Cayo Coco to the mainland. Made of solid earth with only two sluices, it bisects the existing bay and has an impeded tidal flow (see p25).

7 Cayo Romano
MAP L2

Spectacular coral reefs await visitors to this large uninhabited cay. A road connects to the mainland at Brasil, where a military checkpoint sometimes denies access.

8 Fishing

Enthusiasts of fishing can follow the example of Ernest Hemingway who trawled the clear waters off the Jardines del Rey (see p104) for marlin and other game-fish. Sport-fishing trips are offered from the main beach resorts and by Avalon Dive Center.

9 Centro de Investigaciones de Ecosistemas Costeros
MAP K2 ■ Cayo Coco ■ (33) 30 1161

This center for coastal environmental studies and protection is open to the public and features exhibits on manatees, flamingos, and coral reefs.

10 Cayo Anclitas
MAP K4

In the heart of the Jardines de la Reina, this tiny cay has a turtle farm and a visitors' center. A floating hotel offshore plays host to diving and fishing excursions.

Landscape Features

 Mogotes
MAP M4

These dramatic limestone forms (*see p17*) add beauty to the pleasure of hiking in the Área Protegida de Recursos Manejados Sierra del Chorrillo, southeast of Camagüey.

2 Sugarcane Fields
The southern half of the Sancti Spíritus province is a veritable sea of sugarcane, extending east into much of Ciego de Ávila province. Feathery fronds rise from the stalks during the dry summer months.

3 Rugged Mountains
MAP J3 ▪ La Sabina: Carretera Cacahual; (41) 55 4930; ecoturss@ enet.cu

The craggy, thickly forested Alturas de Banao formed a base for Che Guevara's guerrilla army in 1958. Trails lead out from La Sabina, an ecological study camp offering accommodation in rooms and tents.

4 Plains
Hardy cattle munch the windswept, grassy savannah plains of the eastern Ciego de Ávila and Camagüey provinces, where the *vaquero* (cowboy) lifestyle is still very much alive.

5 Lakes
MAP K2 ▪ Morón

Anglers delight in the many fish species near Sancti Spíritus, and in the milky-colored Laguna de la Leche and Lago de Redonda, both outside Morón.

6 Beaches
Sandy beaches unfurl along the Atlantic shore of the Jardines del Rey (*see pp24–5*). The cays of the Jardines de la Reina (*see p104*) are also ringed by white sands. The mainland shore has few beaches (*see pp54–5*).

7 Tropical Forest
MAP L4

Dense montane forests cloak much of this region. Sierra del Chorrillo, south of Camagüey, is an excellent venue for those who want to explore the tropical dry forests.

8 Underground Caves
Caves make up a large part of the limestone uplands around Topes de Collantes (*see p51*). The Cueva del Jabalí at Cayo Coco (*see p107*) features a restaurant and cabaret.

9 Waterfalls
Drenched in rainfall, the Sierra del Escambray around Topes de Collantes (*see p51*) resounds to the thunderous noise of cascades splashing into crystal-clear pools. The Salto de Caburní is easily reached by a well-trodden trail.

10 Coral Cays
Enhanced by their setting in seas of jade and aquamarine, coral cays speckle the oceans off Central Cuba East. Most are uninhabited but offer excellent wildlife viewing.

Coral reef near Cayo Largo

Restaurants

① Mesón de la Plaza
MAP J3 ■ Calle Máximo
Gómez 34, Sancti Spíritus ■ (41) 32
8546 ■ $$

Re-creating the rustic ambience of a
Spanish *bodega* with cowhide chairs
and benches, this restaurant serves
bargain-priced dishes.

Gourmet Restaurant

② Gourmet Restaurant
MAP H4 ■ Calle José Martí 262,
Trinidad ■ (41) 99 6073 ■ $$$

A plush option within the Iberostar
Gran Hotel Trinidad. International
dishes are prepared with aplomb.

③ Vista Gourmet
MAP H4 ■ Callejón Galdos,
Trinidad ■ (41) 99 6700 ■ Open
noon–midnight daily ■ $$

At this attractive *paladar*, you can
enjoy a spectacular dinner buffet
on a rooftop terrace.

④ Guitarra Mía
MAP H4 ■ Calle Jesus
Menéndez 19 between Cienfuegos &
Pérez, Trinidad ■ (41) 99 3452 ■ $$

This homely restaurant serves
delicious *criollo* dishes to the
accompaniment of live music.
The owner is a famous guitarist.

⑤ Restaurante Manacas Iznaga
MAP H4 ■ Iznaga, Valle de los
Ingenios ■ (41) 99 7241 ■ $$

This former sugar-estate owner's
mansion provides a unique setting
for enjoying traditional Cuban dishes.

PRICE CATEGORIES
For a three-course meal with half a bottle
of wine (or equivalent meal), taxes, and
extra charges

$ under CUC$15 $$ CUC$15–25 $$$ over CUC$25

⑥ Fonda Cubana
MAP K3 ■ Calle Máximo
Gómez, Ciego de Ávila ■ (33) 20
0000 ■ Open noon–10pm daily ■ $

Dine on fried chicken, paella, or *ropa
vieja* (shredded beef with vegetables)
on the colonnaded patio of this lovely
colonial building. The fixed-price set
menu is also a bargain.

⑦ Restaurante 1800
MAP L3 ■ Plaza San Juan de
Dios, Camagüey ■ (32) 28 3619 ■ $$

This elegant private restaurant offers
period furnishings, a great location,
and an excellent buffet (menu options
are also available). There are tables
on the attractive square outside.

⑧ Grand Hotel
MAP L3 ■ Calle Maceo 64,
Camagüey ■ (32) 29 2093 ■ $$

Of the Grand Hotel's two choices
of eatery, the rooftop restaurant
is preferred for its quality buffet
dinner. The fine views over the city
center are a definite bonus.

⑨ La Campaña de Toledo
MAP L3 ■ Plaza San Juan
de Dios, Camagüey ■ (32) 28 6812
■ $$

Located in the center of Camagüey,
opposite one of the most emblematic
plazas in the town, this restaurant's
signature dish is *bolice mechado*,
a local beef delicacy.

⑩ Caballo Blanco
MAP M4 ■ Calle Frank País 85,
Las Tunas ■ (31) 34 2586 ■ Open
11am–11pm daily ■ $

One of the finest private restaurants,
this *paladar* features a stone-clad
patio for dining. Try the delicious
chicken with wine and the *ropa vieja*.

See map on pp102–3

ᴛᴏᴘ**10** The Far East

Far-eastern Cuba is dominated by rugged mountains. The Sierra Maestra was the major base of Fidel Castro's guerrilla army *(see p40)*. Sierra Cristal and Sierra Purial are a wilderness of mountain rainforest and offer spectacular hiking and birding. The coastline is no less rugged, with lovely beaches lining the shore of Holguín. Historic cities dot this corner of the republic. Santiago de Cuba *(see pp30–31)* – birthplace of the Revolution – teems with sites of cultural note, while Baracoa is the country's oldest city. Cuba's African heritage is keenly felt in Santiago de Cuba and Guantánamo.

The palm-studded Playa Guardalavaca, Holguín

AREA MAP OF THE FAR EAST

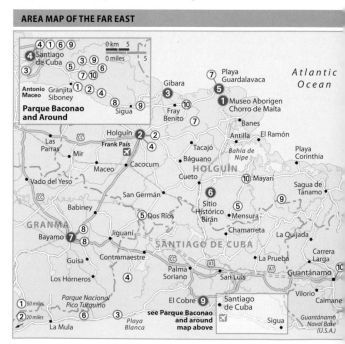

1 Museo Aborigen Chorro de Maíta

MAP P4 ▪ 5 miles (8 km) east of Guardalavaca ▪ (24) 43 0201 ▪ Open 9am–5pm Mon–Sat ▪ Adm

This archaeological site is one of the largest native burial sites in the Caribbean. Of the 108 skeletons unearthed, many still lie in situ as they were found, and can be seen from a boardwalk. A museum displays artifacts. The neighboring Aldea Taína re-creates an Indian village with life-size statues, and the locals re-enact Taíno life.

Sculpture at Museo Aborigen Chorro de Maíta

2 Holguín

Home to colonial plazas, several churches, and museums, this industrious provincial capital is worth exploring (see pp28–9). Its most famous former resident

was Calixto García, a general in the Wars of Independence (see p36). His house, now containing a museum, stands near Plaza Calixto García, where the Museo Provincial de Historia displays period pieces. Climb the steps to the top of Loma de la Cruz for splendid views. Mirador de Mayabe offers a grand mountain-top lunch.

3 Gibara

Once a wealthy port town, Gibara now draws much of its current income from a fishing fleet that harbors in picturesque Bahía de Bariay. The original city walls are now relics, but Parque Calixto García boasts a colonial church and museums of natural history and decorative arts. The town's white-painted houses lend the city its nickname, "Villa Blanca" (White Town) (see p29).

4 Santiago de Cuba

MAP P6 ▪ Casa Museo de Diego Velázquez: Calle Félix Pena 612; (22) 65 2652, 9am–5pm Sat–Thu, 1:30–5pm Fri; adm

Graced by intriguing buildings, this now sprawling industrial city was Cuba's capital until 1553. Must-see sites in its colonial heart include the Cathedral, Casa-Museo de Diego Velázquez, Museo Emilio Bacardí, and the Moncada barracks – a focus for Castro in 1953 (see p37). After the Haitian revolution in 1791, French and Haitian migrants flooded the city and fostered unique forms of architecture, music, and dance. The city is famed for its annual cultural Festival del Pregón in August (see p69).

Museo Emilio Bacardí, Santiago de Cuba

Moa
Cupey
Parque Nacional Alejandro Humboldt
Arroyo Bueno
Felicidad
Zoológico de Piedra
GUANTÁNAMO
San Antonio del Sur
Imías
Baracoa
Maisí
La Máquina
Cajobabo
Punta Caleta
Tortuguilla

0 km   20
0 miles   20

Leisurely street life in Bayamo

5 Playa Guardalavaca

This beach zone, an hour's drive north of Holguín, was developed as a holiday resort in the 1980s and is now Cuba's third-largest resort destination. Development is focused on the beaches of Esmeralda (see p54), Yuraguanal, and Pesquero, and either side of flask-shaped Bahía de Naranjo. The bay has an aquarium, and trails provide insights into local ecology (see p29).

Sitio Histórico Birán

6 Sitio Histórico Birán

MAP N4 ▪ (24) 28 6102 ▪ Open 8am–4pm Tue–Sat (to noon Sun) ▪ Adm (guided tours available)

The Finca Manacas estate, outside Birán, where Fidel Castro was born and lived until his adolescence, belonged to his father Angel Castro (see p40). The wooden mansion has been restored and is furnished with original family pieces. The grounds include Fidel's parents' graves, a former schoolhouse, and buildings, which were relocated to create an idealized village.

7 Bayamo

MAP N5 ▪ Parroquial Mayor de San Salvador: (23) 42 2514; open 9am–11:30am daily; adm ▪ Casa Natal de Carlos Manuel de Céspedes: (23) 42 3864; open 9am–5pm Tue–Fri, 9am–2pm, 8–10pm Sat, 10am–1pm Sun; adm

Founded in 1513 by Diego Velázquez, Bayamo is Cuba's second-oldest city. In the early 19th century it was the cradle of revolt against Spanish rule. Much of the original city was destroyed in 1869, when citizens razed their town rather than surrender to the invading Spanish forces. Fortunately, many key sites survived this destruction, and today the restored historic core is a national monument. Most sights are concentrated around Parque Céspedes and Plaza del Himno, including the not-to-be-missed Parroquial Mayor de San Salvador church and the Casa Natal de Carlos Manuel de Céspedes.

COLUMBUS IN CUBA

Baracoans say that Christopher Columbus (right) landed at Puerto Santo and that the flat-topped mountain he described was El Yunque (see p33). Some experts, however, believe that the mountain was the Silla de Gibara and that Columbus landed in the Bahía de Bariay on October 28, 1492.

8 Zoológico de Piedra
MAP Q5 ■ **Boquerón de Yateras**
■ Open 8am–5pm daily ■ Adm

The name means "stone zoo," a term appropriate for the more than 400 life-size creatures displayed here. The animals, including lions, an elephant, a gorilla, and crocodiles, are carved from stone by coffee farmer Angel Iñigo, a self-taught sculptor who used photographs to hew the creatures. Iñigo has also created entire vignettes such as monkeys picking fleas and Taíno Indians killing a wild boar. The restaurant serves *criollo* meals.

The imposing facade of El Cobre

9 El Cobre
MAP P6 ■ **12 miles (19 km) northwest of Santiago** ■ Sala de Milagros: (22) 34 6118; open 6:30am–6pm

This village is named after the copper (*cobre*) mined here in early colonial days. Pilgrims come to the Basílica de Nuestra Señora de la Caridad del Cobre *(see p31)*, built in 1926, to ask favors of the Virgen de la Caridad, and leave ex votos (offerings) in the Sala de Milagros (Salon of Miracles).

10 Baracoa
Cuba's most easterly city, Baracoa *(see pp32–3)* is spectacularly set within a broad bay. The Hotel El Castillo *(see p129)*, a former fortress, provides the best views in town. The city has a church with a cross that locals believe was brought over by Columbus. Baracoa is a good base for hiking and bird-watching, especially at Parque Nacional Alejandro Humboldt *(see p51)*.

A DRIVE FROM SANTIAGO TO BARACOA

▶ **MORNING**

Leave early from **Santiago de Cuba** *(see p111)*, taking the Autopista Nacional, which begins in the Vista Alegre district. Be careful on the freeway, which has plenty of potholes and traffic. After about 5 miles (8 km), exit at the signed junction for **La Maya**. The road passes through sugarcane fields, with the Sierra Baconao rising to the south. Continue east to **Guantánamo**, where sites of interest around Parque Martí can be explored in one hour. Crossing the Río Bano, divert north to Boquerón de Yateras to reach the **Zoológico de Piedra**, and stop for lunch at the restaurant there.

AFTERNOON

Return to Guantánamo and turn east toward Baracoa. The road passes the entrance to Mirador de Malones and meets the shore at **Playa Yateritas**. At **Cajobabo**, turn south to reach Playita, where a museum recalls José Martí's return from exile. Visit the memorial at the spot where Martí landed with General Máximo Gómez *(see p37)*. Beyond Cajobabo, the road snakes into the Sierra de Purial via **La Farola** *(see p116)*. The mountain road is scenic but drive carefully, especially in fog and rain. At the summit, Alto de Coltillo, have a cup of hot coffee from the roadside shacks before winding back down the mountain's north side toward a coastal plain. Before you arrive in **Baracoa**, make a stop at the small zoo, Parque Zoológico Cacique Guamá *(open 9am–5pm Tue–Sun)*.

See map on pp110–11 ←

Parque Baconao and Around

 Playa Siboney
This pebbly beach frequented by locals has *casas particulares* that offer rooms overlooking the Caribbean *(see p55)*.

 Valle de la Prehistoria
MAP P6 ▪ Carretera de Baconao, km 6.5 ▪ (22) 63 9239 ▪ Open 8am–5pm ▪ Adm
Life-sized model dinosaurs cast in concrete and steel are found at this park *(see p56)*.

3 Jardín Botánico
MAP P6 ▪ Viajes Cubanacán: Av. de las Américas & M, Santiago ▪ (22) 64 2202 ▪ Open 7am–4pm ▪ Adm
Cubanacán offers tours to visit this elevated garden, with flowers that bloom all year round.

4 Museo de Automóviles
MAP P6 ▪ Conjunto de Museos de la Punta, Carretera de Baconao, km 8.5 ▪ (22) 63 9197 ▪ Open 8am–5pm ▪ Adm
Among the cars on display is the curious one-cylinder Maya Cuba. An adjoining museum displays around 2,500 toy cars.

 Prado de las Esculturas
MAP P6 ▪ Carretera a Siboney & Carretera de la Gran Piedra ▪ Open 8am–4pm ▪ Adm
A walking trail leads past metal artworks in this sculpture garden.

 Cafetal La Isabelica
MAP P6 ▪ Carretera de la Gran Piedra, km 14 ▪ Open 8am–4pm ▪ Adm
Learn about coffee production at this 18th-century coffee estate.

7 Museo de la Guerra Hispano-Cubano-Norteamericano
MAP P6 ▪ Carretera Siboney, km 13 ▪ (22) 39 9119 ▪ Open 9am–5pm Mon–Sat ▪ Adm
This museum has original weaponry and uniforms from the 1898 Spanish-American War *(see p47)*.

8 Comunidad Artística Los Mamoncillos
MAP Q6 ▪ Playa Verraco, Carretera de Baconao
Shop for original works at this hamlet dedicated to arts and crafts.

 Acuario Baconao
MAP Q6 ▪ Carretera de Baconao, km 47 ▪ (22) 35 6176 ▪ Open 9am–4pm Tue–Sun ▪ Adm
This aquatic park puts on dolphin shows twice daily.

10 Granita Siboney
MAP P6 ▪ Carretera Siboney, km 13 ▪ (22) 39 9168 ▪ Open 9am–5pm daily (to 1pm Mon) ▪ Adm
Fidel Castro and his revolutionaries set out from this farmstead on July 26, 1953, to attack Moncada barracks *(see p37)*. A museum tells the tale.

Prado de las Esculturas

Things to Do

(1) Visit Cayo Saetía
MAP P4 ▪ (24) 51 6900
African game roam freely in the wilds of this small island with sensational white beaches. It was once a hunting preserve for the Communist elite.

(2) Dive at Marea del Portillo
MAP M6 ▪ Albacora Dive Center: Marea del Portillo ▪ (23) 59 7139
This otherwise modest beach resort will thrill scuba aficionados with its splendid dive sites. The highlight is the wreck of the Spanish warship, *Cristóbal Colón*, sunk in 1898.

Pristine beaches at Cayo Saetía island

(3) Drive to Chivirico
MAP M6–P6
Soaring skyward from a teal-blue sea, the Sierra Maestra push up against a barren coast road linking Marea del Portillo with Santiago de Cuba. The stunning scenery is the perfect backdrop to the road.

(4) Dance at the Casa de la Trova, Santiago
The epicenter of *son* music (see p58), Casa de la Trova has been a center of learning for top musicians. Paintings of famous artists adorn the walls.

(5) Honor José Martí at Dos Ríos
MAP N5
The site of José Martí's martyrdom (see p37) is marked by an obelisk. The memorial, surrounded by white roses, is an allusion to Martí's famous poem, *Cultivo una rosa blanca*.

(6) Hiking in Parque Nacional Desembarco del Granma
The site of the *Granma* landing (see p38), this park features trails through semi-arid forest with caves. Marine terraces offer great views (see p51).

(7) Boat Ride at Yumurí
MAP R5
The Río Yumurí runs through coastal mountains and is a stunning setting for boat trips departing from the wharf at the river mouth. Negotiate a fee with the boat owners first.

(8) Spot Manatees at Parque Nacional Alejandro Humboldt
MAP R5 ▪ Ecotur: Calle Maceo 120, Baracoa ▪ (21) 64 3665
Guided boat trips, arranged through Ecotur, offer passengers the chance for a rare encounter with the endearing and endangered manatees, as they paddle around in the mangrove-lined waters of Bahía de Taco bay.

(9) Birding in Sierra Cristal
Sightings of colorful Cuban parrots and *tocororos* (see p52) are the rewards for bird enthusiasts on hikes through the montane forests of northeastern Cuba.

(10) Steam Train Ride
Hop onto an antique steam train at Rafael Freyre for a scenic tour of the Grupo Maniabón mountains (see p116). Tours can be arranged through hotel desks in Guardalavaca and Holguín.

See map on pp110–11 ←

Mountain Highs

El Yunque, Baracoa

1 El Yunque

A unique flat top on El Yunque forms a dramatic backdrop to Baracoa, and you can hike to the summit. The views from the top are fabulous and worth the trip *(see p33)*.

2 La Farola
MAP R5

Experience a winding, breathtakingly steep drive up the mountain linking Guantánamo to Baracoa. Magnificent scenery awaits drivers, but extreme care is required on the way up.

3 Parque Nacional Alejandro Humboldt
MAP R5 ■ Ecotur: (21) 64 3665

Don sturdy footwear for the hike into the mountains of this park, which features *miradores* (lookouts) offering marvelous views. Guides are mandatory, and Ecotur can arrange them for you.

4 El Saltón
MAP N5 ■ Villa El Saltón: (22) 56 6326

This ecotourism mountain resort offers trails, waterfalls, and superb bird-watching. The Villa El Saltón is a good base for exploring.

5 Pinares de Mayarí
MAP P5 ■ (24) 45 5628

Accessed by a denuded road, this mountain resort *(see p51)* offers outdoor activities amid the pine forests, as well as around the Salto el Guayabo waterfall.

6 Parque Nacional Pico Turquino
MAP N6

Cuba's highest peak *(see p51)* is a challenging two-day ascent leading through various ecosystems, including a cloud forest.

7 Grupo Maniabón
MAP P4

Surrounded by *mogotes (see p17)*, this visually delightful mountain chain northeast of Holguín is best explored via a steam train excursion.

8 La Comandancia de la Plata

Fidel Castro's former guerrilla headquarters, hidden by thick forest and overhanging a ravine, are kept as they were five decades ago *(see p39)*.

9 Gran Piedra
MAP P6

The "Great Stone" is a huge boulder balanced atop the ridge of the Sierra Baconao, and reached via a 454-step staircase. It offers panoramic views, and Haiti can be seen on the horizon.

10 Mayarí Arriba
MAP P6 ■ Museo Comandancia del Segundo Frente: Av. de los Mártires, Santiago de Cuba; (22) 42 5749; open 9am–4:30pm Tue–Sat, 9am–noon Sun

The Museo Comandancia del Segundo Frente recalls the years of the Revolution when the pine forests surrounding this town were the setting for guerrilla warfare.

Restaurants

1 Paladar Salón Tropical
MAP P6 ■ Calle Luis Fernándes Marcané 310 Altos, Santiago de Cuba ■ (22) 64 1161 ■ $

The best *paladar* (private restaurant) in Santiago serves mixed grills and seafood on its terrace. The menu ranges from pizza to lamb stew.

2 Restaurante 1720
MAP N4 ■ Calle Frexes 190, Holguín ■ (24) 46 8150 ■ $$

Located in a restored colonial mansion, Restaurante 1720 offers a creative menu that includes paella, and tasty creole shrimp in rum.

3 Restaurante El Morro
MAP P6 ■ Parque Histórico El Morro, Santiago de Cuba ■ (22) 69 1576 ■ $$

This delightfully rustic restaurant sits atop a coastal headland. Eat your *criolla* lunch while enjoying the spectacular views from the terrace.

Restaurante El Morro

4 Restaurante Loma de la Cruz
MAP N4 ■ Loma de la Cruz, Holguín ■ (24) 47 1523 ■ $$

Incomparable views over the city are offered at the Spanish *bodega*-style place. Try the tasty lamb enchilada.

5 El Poeta
MAP R5 ■ Calle Maceo 159, Baracoa ■ (21) 64 3017 ■ $

This charming *paladar* is set in a wooden house. The ebullient owner

will sing impromptu poetry as you dine on creative dishes that are unique to the region.

6 El Barracón
MAP P6 ■ Av. Victoriano Garzón, Santiago de Cuba ■ (22) 66 1877 ■ $

At this rustic restaurant diners sit at long tables to enjoy dishes such as *carne pa' changó*, a spicy stew.

7 Restaurant La Maison
MAP P4 ■ Playa Mayor, Guardalavaca ■ (24) 48 0839 ■ $

Have an elaborate meal of lobster and *paella* at great prices at this clifftop restaurant offering fine scenery.

8 Paladar La Estrella
MAP N5 ■ General García between Masó & Lora, Bayamo ■ (23) 42 3950 ■ $

Sample reasonably priced, good *criolla* staples, such as garlic shrimp, at this private restaurant.

9 Restaurante Zunzún
MAP P6 ■ Av. Manduley 159, Santiago de Cuba ■ (22) 64 1528 ■ $$

This atmospheric eatery has a wide-ranging menu. Housed in a colonial mansion, you can enjoy your meal in the comfort of the air-conditioned salon or on the terrace outside.

10 Ranchón El Gobernador
MAP Q5 ■ Glorieta, 13 miles (21 km) E of Guantánamo ■ Open 24 hrs ■ $

This breeze-swept hilltop restaurant serves simple dishes, but its appeal also lies in its fabulous views over Guantánamo Bay.

See map on pp110–11

Streetsmart

Classic American car in Trinidad

Getting To and Around Cuba

Airlines

Virgin Atlantic offers regular flights between London and Havana. Air France, Iberia, and KLM fly from Europe to Cuba, as do charter companies such as Air Europa, Air Berlin, and Thomson. Air Canada, Cubana, and many charter companies connect Canada with the island. No US airlines fly direct to Cuba, other than charter companies for licensed travelers, but in 2015 negotiations began to relax restrictions, and commercial flights for tourists from the US may be allowed in the future.

Fares are lower off-season, which runs from May to November, and for mid-week departures. As far as possible, it is best to book in advance. Charter companies are usually cheaper than scheduled airlines, although more restrictions apply.

Arriving by Air

Situated on the southern outskirts of Havana, **Aeropuerto Internacional José Martí** is the main entrance for visitors to the capital. There is no bus service; travelers will need to take a taxi for the 30-minute ride into the city. You should agree the fare with the driver in advance – it should be about CUC$20–25.

The **Aeropuerto Internacional Antonio Maceo** is about 5 miles (8 km) south of Santiago de Cuba's center. Bus services are unreliable, and the best bet is to take a taxi. Official tourist taxis should cost about CUC$8–10, and you must agree the fare with the driver in advance to avoid paying over the odds later.

There are also international airports at Varadero, Ciego de Ávila, Cayo Coco, Cienfuegos, Santa Clara, Camagüey (for Playa Santa Lucía), and Holguín (for the resorts of Guardalavaca), and Cayo Largo.

All visitors must present a tourist card at Cuban immigration upon arrival. The card costs around CUC$25 and is valid for 30 days; Canadians get one for 90 days. Cards are issued when you purchase or check in for a flight to Cuba, and must be shown at passport control.

Tourist taxis are present at international airports. As few taxi drivers use meters, it is customary to agree a fare before setting off. Touts may attempt to steer you toward private taxis, but always decline the offer.

It is impossible to obtain Cuban Convertible Pesos (see p123) outside Cuba, so exchange currency on arrival in Cuba. CADECA (see p124) offers money-changing services at the main airports.

Arriving by Ship

A few Caribbean-based cruise lines include Cuba in their itineraries, calling in at the port facilities of Havana and, less frequently, Santiago de Cuba and Cienfuegos. In 2015, the US government began licensing US cruise lines for "people-to-people" cruises.

Marinas around the island act as official ports of entry for independent sailors. However, US sailors currently require prior approval from the Coast Guard and the Office of Foreign Assets Control (OFAC).

Traveling by Air

Cubana de Aviación has regular connections between Havana, the provincial capitals, and key tourist centers around the island. Although these can be useful, demand often exceeds supply and services are unreliable. The code-linked **Aerocaribbean** airline also offers some services.

Traveling by Bus

A reliable long-distance bus service is provided by **Víazul**. It connects Havana to provincial capitals and major tourist destinations. The buses are air-conditioned with restrooms. Online booking is possible. Non-Cubans are barred from the Omnibus Nacionales system.

Guaguas are local buses that are usually packed to the brim with passengers. *Camellos* (camels) – the local name for cramped articulated buses pulled by lorries – have been replaced by metro buses in Havana, but they still operate in provincial cities.

BusTour is an open-top double-decker tour bus operating in ten key locations islandwide, with a hop-on/hop-off service at stops en route.

Traveling by Car

Car rental is widely available, but expensive. All rental agencies are government owned. Responsibility of the car maintenance is placed on the renters by contract. **Rex** is the most reputable company but also the least cost-effective.

Driving can be quite a challenge due to poor roads, a lack of signs, and numerous obstacles. Poor street lighting makes night-driving hazardous. *Tránsito* (traffic police) enforce speed limits of 30 mph (40 km/h) in towns, 37 mph (59 km/h) on rural roads, 55 mph (88 km/h) on highways, and 62 mph (98 km/h) on freeways.

Traveling by Rail

Cuba has 3,030 miles (4,876 km) of public railroads, serving all the provincial capitals. Branch lines extend to other cities, while small commuter trains provide service to some Havana suburbs and provincial towns.

The Ferrocarriles Nacionales de Cuba operates the dysfunctional train service using aged and usually unclean carriages. Schedules change frequently, trains rarely operate on time, and cancellations are common. An effort to modernize the system was initiated in 2010, including new Chinese locomotives. "Especiales," which cover the Havana–Santiago route, have air-conditioning, reclinable seats and a somewhat limited and sporadic refreshment service. Buying a ticket through the **FerroCuba** state agency can be tricky.

Havana's principle train station closed in June 2015 for a three-year renovation. Most trains now depart from Le Coubre terminal, while those for Cienfuegos and Pinar del Río depart from the 19 de Noviembre (Tulipán) terminal.

Traveling by Taxi

There is no shortage of taxis in the main tourist areas. However, most drivers do not use their meters so as to negotiate a fare. Cocotaxis are egg-shaped, bright yellow scooters; they cost the same as a regular taxi and work well for short distances but are not as safe. Shared *colectivo* or peso taxis can be used by foreigners; they operate on fixed routes.

Bicitaxis – crude bicycle-rickshaws – are a staple means of getting around within cities. They provide a fun, but slow, way to travel short distances.

Antique horse-drawn carriages are a good way of sightseeing in Old Havana, Varadero, and a few other cities.

Getting Around on Foot

Cuba's compact colonial city centers are perfect for exploring on foot. Licensed guides can be hired in Old Havana, Trinidad, and Santiago de Cuba. Beware of hustlers selling tours on the street, as they cannot be trusted.

DIRECTORY

INTERNATIONAL AIRPORTS

Antonio Maceo
Santiago de Cuba
(22) 69 8614

Cayo Coco
(33) 30 9165

Frank País
Holguín
(24) 46 2512

Ignacio Agramonte
Camagüey
(32) 26 1010

José Martí
Havana
7266 4133

Juan Gualberto Gómez
Varadero
(45) 24 7015

Máximo Gómez
Ciego de Ávila
(33) 22 5717

US GOVERNMENT OFFICES

Office of Foreign Assets
treas.gov/ofac

LOCAL AIRLINES

Aerocaribbean
7832 7584

Cubana de Aviación
Calle 23 No. 64, Havana
7834 4446
cubana.cu

BUS SERVICES

BusTour
7835 0000
transtur.cu

Víazul
7881 1413
viazul.com

CAR RENTAL

Rex
rex.cu

Transtur
transturcarrental.com

RAIL

FerroCuba
7861-9389 or 861-8540

Practical Information

Passports and Visas

All visitors must have a valid passport, a tourist card (see p120), health insurance, and an onward ticket. It is wise to photo-copy passport details. US law currently allows its citizens to visit Cuba if they fall into one of twelve categories under a general (pre-authorized) license from the OFAC (see pp120–21).

Customs Regulations and Immigration

Visitors are allowed to bring in 200 cigarettes and 6 pints (3 liters) of spirits duty free, plus 44 lb (20 kg) of personal belongings into the country. Certain electronic items are prohibited, and Customs is sensitive to visitors arriving with cellphones, cameras, or computer storage devices. Customs searches in Cuba can be rigorous, and the authorities take a harsh line on drugs.

Travel Safety Advice

Visitors can get up-to-date travel safety information from the **Foreign and Commonwealth Office** in the UK, the **State Department** in the US, and the **Department of Foreign Affairs and Trade** in Australia.

Travel Insurance

Medical insurance is now obligatory when visiting Cuba, as any illness or accident may involve paying for treatment. It is also worth having insurance against loss or theft of valuables. Visitors intending to engage in any form of extreme sports during their trip should ensure that they are covered.

When to Go

Cuba's tourist season runs from December to April, when airfares, accommodations, and car rentals are at their most expensive. This period is less hot than the rest of the year, but temperatures in January can reach 79°F (26°C). The hurricane season lasts from June to November, with the majority of storms occurring in September and October.

Most visitors to Cuba arrive for beach vacations of a week to 10 days. Havana itself requires at least four days to fully explore, while Viñales, Trinidad, and Santiago de Cuba deserve two each. Allow at least three to four weeks to explore the length of Cuba, from Pinar del Río to Baracoa.

What to Take

Light cotton clothing is recommended. Bring swimwear for a beach holiday, as it can be expensive in Cuba. It is worth packing a sweater or lightweight jacket for heavily air-conditioned restaurants, chilly winter nights, and visits to mountainous regions. Long-sleeved clothing and mosquito repellent help guard against mosquitoes. Sunscreen, a hat, and sunglasses are also essential items.

Time Zone

Cuba is on Eastern Standard Time (EST) and is 5 hours behind Greenwich Mean Time (GMT), the same as New York and Miami. Daylight saving time operates from May to October.

Electricity

Cuba's erratic electricity supply works on a 110-volt system, as in the US and Canada, although some outlets are 220-volt and are usually marked. Plugs are the two-pin North American type, so European visitors will need to bring adaptors.

Opening Hours

Most offices are open 8:30am–12:30pm and 1:30–5:30pm Monday to Friday. Shops usually remain open 8:30am–5:30pm Monday to Saturday. Banks typically open 8:30am–noon and 1:30–3pm Monday to Friday, and then 8:30–10:30am on Saturdays. Museums hours vary widely, but bear in mind that many are closed on Mondays.

Sources of Information

Official Cuban tourist offices in Canada and the United Kingdom provide basic information on the country. For more specific details, it is better to contact independent agencies. US citizens planning a visit should contact the Cubatur office in Canada.

Cuban websites are all state-run, and care should be taken if booking online. US websites are now permitted to accept bookings for trips to Cuba. *La Habana* is an online magazine with a monthly "What's On" downloadable brochure.

Infotur tourist offices are scattered throughout major tourist centers, but few have the resources to answer more than the most basic questions.

Cuba's larger tour operators can provide information on specific regions and activities, but their knowledge is often limited and unreliable. It is better to seek out smaller operators who can offer more specialized tours.

Government-run tour operators can provide guides, and many taxi drivers also act as driver-guides. Car-rental agencies will provide a driver-guide on request. Many individuals offer legal freelance services, but exercise caution when hiring them.

TV, Radio, and Newspapers

All branches of Cuban media are state controlled. The government's official newspaper, *Granma*, is published in English and distributed at hotels. There are two other newspapers, *Juventud Rebelde* and *Trabajadores*. Foreign publications are not sold

in Cuba. Most tourist hotels have satellite TV showing CNN and a selection of English-language news stations, although Cuban homes receive only local state-run stations.

Maps and Guides

A few bookstores in Havana and some shops in large tourist hotels sell a limited range of maps, books, and other travel-related literature. There are very few outlets elsewhere. A second-hand book sale is held daily on Havana's Plaza de Armas *(see p72)*.

There are several good maps of the country; the best are the National Geographic Adventure Maps. In Cuba, tourist outlets sell a tourist map of Havana published by Ediciones Geo, and *Guía de Carreteras*, an excellent road atlas.

Currency

The Cuban national peso (CUP) is made of 100 *centavos*. The peso is used mostly by Cubans; there are very few places where tourists will be able, or wish, to use pesos except local buses, baseball stadiums, and food stalls on the street.

All tourist transactions and major purchases are conducted in Cuban Convertible Pesos *(pesos convertibles)*, designated as CUC$, with bills of 1, 3, 5, 10, 20, 50, and 100. The value is pegged at US$1.00 and CUP24. However, it has no value outside Cuba. Euros can be used in Varadero, Cayo Coco, and Cayo Largo.

DIRECTORY

LOCAL TOURIST OFFICES
Infotur
℡ 7204 0624
🖳 infotur.cu

TRAVEL SAFETY ADVICE
Australia
Department of Foreign Affairs and Trade
🖳 dfat.gov.au/
🖳 smarttraveller.gov.au/

UK
Foreign and Commonwealth Office
🖳 gov.uk/foreign-travel-advice

US
US Department of State
🖳 travel.state.gov/

WEBSITES AND BOOKSTORES
La Habana
🖳 lahabana.com

Libreria La Moderna Poesia
MAP V5 ■ Calle Obispo 525, La Habana Vieja
℡ /861 6640

EMBASSIES AND CONSULATES
Canada
MAP D2 ■ Calle 30 518, Havana ℡ 7204 2516

UK
MAP D2 ■ Calle 34 702, Havana ℡ 7214 2200

US
MAP T1 ■ Calzada & L, Havana ℡ 7839 4100

MAJOR PUBLIC HOLIDAYS
Jan 1
Liberation Day

Jan 2
Victory Day

Jul 26
National Revolution Day

Oct 10
Independence Day

Dec 25
Christmas Day

Banks and ATMs

All banks in Cuba are state-owned. Most will exchange foreign currency at the official rate, though queuing can be quite a lengthy operation. The regular opening hours are normally 8am–3pm Monday to Friday, but some banks are also open on Saturday mornings. Some ATMs in major towns can be used to obtain cash advances using cards such as MasterCard and Visa, except for those that have been issued or processed by any US institutions.

Foreign currency can be exchanged for CUC$ and CUPs at CADECA *casas de cambio* (bureaux de change). A 10 percent commission is charged if you would like to change US dollars; however, no such commissions exist for other currencies.

Credit Cards

MasterCard and Visa are widely accepted in hotels, restaurants, and tourist-oriented stores, but not in out-of-the-way places and smaller outlets. Cards issued by US banks can be used, but may not work. Be prepared for the electronic processing system to be unreliable. Credit cards can be used in order to obtain cash advances at certain banks. An 11 percent commission is charged for using credit cards.

Communications

Operated by ETECSA, a state company, public phones are plentiful and normally reliable. Public phones work with prepaid phone cards for between CUC$5 and CUC$50. These allow you to make relatively inexpensive international calls from any public telephone. Making calls from hotels can be quite expensive.

Cubacel is the cell phone service provider and has offices in most major cities and tourist centers. If you bring your personal cell phone, Cubacel may be able to activate it, but it is expensive.

Local area codes may have 1 or 2 digits, and the number of digits of local numbers varies. To call outside Cuba, dial 119, followed by the country code. To call Cuba from abroad, dial the international access number (00 in the UK, 011 in the US and Canada), then 53 and the local number.

Mail is extremely slow. Every town has a post office, and most tourist hotels also sell stamps or prepaid postcards. All mail is read by censors. If sending anything of value or importance, use DHL, which has offices in all major cities.

Laptops for personal use may be brought into Cuba. You can log onto the Internet in many hotels and a few cyber cafés. However, the cost can vary widely. Private Internet access for Cubans is limited to a privileged few. Wi-Fi is very limited.

Emergencies

The Cuban police are rarely very responsive to reports of crimes against tourists, and reporting a theft can result in a lengthy bureaucratic procedure. Every town and village has its own police station but few officers speak English. If you are a victim of theft or are involved in an accident, the best course of action is to contact your embassy or consulate, which should be able to help you *(see p123)*. You should also contact your embassy or consulate for help immediately if you are arrested.

Asistur exists to help tourists in distress and has offices in most tourist centers. The **Consultoría Jurídica Internacional** can provide legal help and has branches in all of Cuba's main cities.

In the event of a car accident, call the traffic police *(tránsito)* and your car-rental company. It is also wise to contact your embassy immediately. Do not allow any vehicle that has been involved in an accident to be moved before the police arrive.

Canada, the UK, and most European nations have embassies in Havana with consular services, as does the US since August 2015. All can provide assistance to travelers.

Medical Services

Cuba's healthcare system is free of charge to Cubans. Foreign visitors are usually treated in international clinics; emergency treatment is provided at ordinary hospitals, but hygiene is usually questionable. Payment is made in convertible pesos or by credit card, but fees are relatively inexpensive.

Most tourist hotels will also have a doctor or nurse on call.

Pharmaceuticals are in short supply, except in *farmacias internacionales*, found in major cities and resorts. It is advisable to bring your own supply of medicines you require, as well as any prescriptions you have for these, and plenty of sunscreen and insect repellent.

Personal Safety

Violent crime against foreigners is rare, but in tourist areas and run-down sections of Havana, there is always a risk of pick-pocketing and bag-snatching. Avoid dark and lonely spots, do not carry large amounts of cash, or flaunt expensive items. Theft from hotel rooms is a common occurrence, so keep your possessions locked in your bag and your valuables in a safe.

Visitors in well-trodden tourist areas may well experience some level of harassment from individuals offering a range of services. *Jineteros* (male hustlers) will attempt to sell you fake cigars as the real thing; *jineteras* are female prostitutes. The best way to deal with either is simply to ignore them.

Cubans hitchhike from necessity due to the poor public transportation system, although officials discourage tourists from hitchhiking or offering lifts. Foreign embassies in Cuba report an increasing number of robberies by Cuban hitchhikers.

Cuba's government has a history of repressing homosexuality. However,

it is now becoming increasingly lenient and even supportive. Unfortunately, police harassment of homo-sexuals still occurs.

Women Travelers

Female tourists can receive a fair amount of unwanted attention from Cuban men, which, for the most part, takes the form of verbal intrusions. The most effective response to them is a stony glare or cold indifference.

Despite advances in women's rights, *machismo* is ingrained in Cuba's male culture. This is generally limited to flirtatious behavior toward women but can also include expressions of bravado and even aggression intended to demonstrate male pride.

Health and Hygiene

Do not drink the tap water. Some people prefer not to brush their teeth with it. You should also make sure that ice cubes are made from purified water. Bottled water can be bought cheaply and is widely available. Do not drink from a bottle of water that is unsealed, as it may have been refilled with tap water.

The best way to avoid an upset stomach is to steer clear of certain foods, notably lobster and shrimp dishes. Also do not eat meats or dairy products that have been allowed to stand too long on a buffet counter or in the sun. Food from street stalls should be avoided.

It is easy to become dehydrated in Cuba's warm climate, where sweat often evaporates immediately. Drink plenty of bottled water and watch out for headaches, exhaustion, and muscle cramps – signs that you may be suffering from dehydration or heatstroke.

Do not underestimate the power of the tropical sun. Sunburn and sunstroke are the most common health problems tourists encounter when visiting Cuba. Avoid the hottest part of the day, between noon and 3pm, and use a strong sun-screen, even when the weather is cloudy.

DIRECTORY

EMERGENCIES

Ambulance
(104

Fire Service
(105

Police
(106

POLICE STATION

Havana
MAP X2 ■ Calle Picota
(7867 0496

ASISTUR

Havana
MAP W1 ■ Paseo de Martí 208 (7866 4499

Santiago de Cuba
MAP P6 ■ Hotel Casagranda ((22) 68 6128 W asistur.cu

Varadero
MAP F1 ■ Calle 30 e/ 1ra y 3ra
((45) 66 7277

LEGAL ASSISTANCE

Consultoría Jurídica Internacional
MAP D2 ■ Calle 16 314, Miramar, Havana
(7204 2490 W cji.co.cu

Culture and Etiquette

Cubans generally dress informally but are usually smartly turned out. Top restaurants require trousers as opposed to jeans or shorts for men. A collared shirt is a good idea for meetings.

It is common courtesy to ask permission before taking a photograph of any individual, but this especially applies to members of the police and military personnel. Photographing industrial complexes, airports, ports, and military installations is strictly prohibited.

Cuba enjoys harmonious relations between races, and mixed-race marriages are common. However, racism has not been entirely eradicated, and black youths are the most likely targets.

Civility is important to Cubans, who greet everyone in a room when entering. Women will embrace and kiss each other's cheeks, while men shake hands. Common greetings that you will hear (and ideally use) everywhere are *buenos días* (good morning), *buenas tardes* (good afternoon), and *buenas noches* (good evening).

The Cuban government is highly sensitive to criticism of the Cuban system. Secret police and informers are ubiquitous. For this reason, Cubans are extremely wary about discussing politics with people they do not know or trust. Avoid drawing people into conversations about politics, except in private, and foreigners should avoid making critical statements in public. Any tourist who meets with dissidents or visits "independent libraries" is also likely to face problems with the Cuban authorities.

Bureaucracy pervades every aspect of Cuban life involving the State. Most services oriented toward tourism function fluidly, although unbending regulations can make dealing with businesses and especially government institutions an extremely frustrating experience.

Dining

Long gone are the days when visitors justifiably complained about stodgy cuisine and boring menus. Standards have improved vastly since 2011, when Raúl Castro ended most restrictions on private restaurants and initiated reforms in farming and food sales. Havana has experienced a culinary revolution of sorts, with scores of new *paladares* (private restaurants), many of them world-class. It's now possible to dine well every day of the week on globe-spanning menus, although the most consistently rewarding dining is still often found in restaurants that specialize in Cuban fare. Even many of the state-run restaurants have improved. Some *paladares* wouldn't seem out of place in New York or London for their chic ambiance; others, such as Havana's La Guarida *(see p79)* occupy gorgeous but dilapidated buildings. And private restaurants specializing in pizza and burgers (of vastly varying quality) are now numerous.

No community in Cuba is now without at least one *paladar*, including the beach resorts, such as Varadero, where private restaurants had been previously banned. Trinidad has also seen an explosion of quality *paladares*. Virtually everywhere beyond Havana, *paladares* tend to be packed with locals. Dishes are often simple, but always filling and usually of surprisingly high quality – and almost always better than the state-run restaurants, which the government intends eventually to eliminate entirely.

Beach resort hotels usually have a choice of restaurants offering international cuisine and the option of à la carte or smorgasbord-style buffet dining (know as *mesa sueca*, meaning "Swiss buffet"), usually included in your all-inclusive rate.

Budget travelers will find all manner of snacks sold at cafés and streetside stalls. Almost all of these sell the ubiquitous ham and cheese *bocadito* (sandwich) and/or simple *cajita* (boxed lunches). Caution should be used when buying food items at streetside stalls, where hygiene may be questionable. When buying ice cream, stick to Coppelia – the state-run chain, with outlets in most major cities – or Nestlé, sold in shops nationwide. Every community has at least one *agromercado* (produce market), where you can buy fresh fruit and vegetables for pesos.

Shopping

Rum and cigars are readily available, but should be bought only in state-run **Casa del Habano** outlets, some of which are attached to Havana's factories that make cigars for export. Do not buy cigars from *jineteros* (touts) on the street; their wares will almost certainly be fakes or flawed.

Cuban music CDs can be bought at **ARTex** stores, often to be found in hotel lobbies, but touts also sell bootleg copies of variable quality on the street.

Opening hours for state-run *tiendas* (stores) are typically 9am–5pm, although some stay open longer. On Sundays, shops close at 1pm.

Accommodation

Quality varies markedly at all-inclusive hotels, but in general you get what you pay for. The buffet may get monotonous, and alcohol is limited to national brands of rum and beer, with watered-down wine for dinner. In theory, everything is included in your room rate, but check in advance to see what extra charges may apply. In general, those managed by foreign companies are of a higher standard than the locally managed all-inclusives.

Renting a room in a private home *(see p133)* is rewarding for visitors who want to experience everyday Cuban family life. Conditions at *casas particulares* can be fairly simple, but the cost is less than hotels, and the experience is authentic. Recent years have seen a tremedous increase in the number of *casas particulares*, including many relatively deluxe homes, some of which can be rented in their entirety and may have as many as five or more bedrooms. Home-cooked meals are often available for a little extra. Most *casas particulares* will accept unmarried couples. Licensed room rentals are identified by an official blue marker resembling an inverted anchor. In Havana, rentals range from CUC$25–60 per room per night, depending on quality. Homes rented in their entirety typically range from CUC$100–400 nightly. In the provinces such rentals are considerably cheaper, with some budget properties for as low as CUC$15 per room per night.

Almost every hotel and *casa particular* offers air conditioning. Large tourist hotels have a back-up generator, but smaller hotels will often suffer blackouts. Some hotels also have ceiling fans, and *casa particular* owners will usually provide a standing fan if you request one.

Most hotels can be booked online through the state-run hotel chain websites, although it is usually more reliable to use the websites of foreign hotel chains, such as **Iberostar** and **Meliá**, which manage the hotels. Many *casas particulares* have their own websites, and/or are represented by websites such as **Airbnb** and **MyCasaParticular**. Since 2015, licensed US travelers may now legally use such websites to make reservations.

Very few hotels have facilities for the disabled, although recently built or renovated hotels usually have at least one room that is equipped for disabled travelers. Cuban society is very caring towards disabled people, and hotel managers will try to make their stay as comfortable as possible.

Tipping is customary for hotel staff, although it is at your own discretion. Tip porters CUC$1 per bag carried to your room. If you leave CUC$1 daily in your room you are less likely to experience theft of personal items by housekeepers.

Most large tourist hotels have adequate parking facilities for rental cars. However, smaller inner-city hotels and *casas particulares* rarely do. In such cases, enquire about a secure parking lot that is well guarded, to ensure the safety of your vehicle.

DIRECTORY

SHOPPING

ARTex
Ⓦ artexsa.com/tiendas

Casa del Habano
Ⓦ lacasadel
habano.com

ACCOMMODATION

Airbnb
Ⓦ airbnb.com

Iberostar
Ⓦ iberostar.com

Meliá
Ⓦ meliacuba.com

MyCasaParticular
Ⓦ mycasa
particular.com

Places to Stay

PRICE CATEGORIES

For a standard double room per night (with breakfast if included), taxes, and extra charges.

$ under CUC$50 $$ CUC$50–150 $$$ over CUC$150

Havana Hotels

Hostal Los Frailes

MAP X2 ■ Calle Brasil between Oficios & Mercaderes, La Habana Vieja ■ 7862 9383 ■ www. habaguanex.ohc.cu ■ $$
Themed as a monastery with staff that dress as monks, this hotel has cozy rooms with wrought-iron furnishings surrounding a patio. There is no restaurant, but nearby Plaza Vieja has several options.

Hotel Raquel

MAP X2 ■ Amargura & San Ignacio, La Habana Vieja ■ 7860 8280 ■ www. habaguanex.ohc.cu ■ $$
A stylish historic hotel with Art Nouveau decor and an excellent location just one block from Plaza Vieja. Facilities include a solarium and a gym.

Hotel Capri

MAP U1 ■ Calle 21 esq. N, Vedado ■ 7839 7200 ■ www.gran-caribe.cu ■ $$$
Reopened in 2014 after a five-year renovation, this historic hotel with mobster associations now gleams afresh. Modern amenities include Wi-Fi and a club.

Hotel Conde de Villanueva

MAP X4 ■ Calle Mercaderes 202, La Habana Vieja ■ 7862 9293 ■ www. habaguanex.ohc.cu ■ $$$
In the heart of La Habana Vieja, the former mansion of the Count of Villanueva offers nine intimate rooms facing an airy courtyard. A cigar lounge draws serious smokers.

Hotel Florida

MAP X1 ■ Calle Obispo 252, La Habana Vieja ■ 7862 4127 ■ www. habaguanex.ohc.cu ■ $$$
A magnificent colonial building and a haven of peace on La Habana Vieja's busiest street, this sumptuous hotel is centered on a courtyard. It has spacious rooms furnished in colonial style with wrought-iron beds.

Hotel Iberostar Parque Central

MAP W1 ■ Calle Neptuno between Prado & Zulueta ■ 7860 6627 ■ www. iberostar.com ■ $$$
This luxury option overlooks Havana's liveliest square with elegant rooms that feature reproduction antiques and Wi-Fi connections. It has a classy lobby bar, two fine restaurants, boutiques, and a rooftop swimming pool. Popular with tour groups.

Hotel Nacional

MAP U1 ■ Calle O & 21, Vedado ■ 7836 3564 ■ www.hotelnacionalde cuba.com ■ $$$
Built in the 1930s, this gracious grande-dame is considered to be Havana's top hotel. It offers four restaurants and six bars, including a lovely garden terrace bar and the Cabaret Parisien, as well as two large swimming pools. Many rooms are dowdy, so take an executive floor room.

Hotel Saratoga

MAP W1 ■ Paseo de Martí 603, La Habana Vieja ■ 7868 1000 ■ www. hotel-saratoga.com ■ $$$
The most sophisticated hotel in town, this stylish restoration of a historic hotel merges colonial and ultra-contemporary features. Rooms have DVD players, Wi-Fi connections, and posh furnishings. A fabulous restaurant, chic bar, and rooftop pool complete the picture.

Hotel Tryp Habana Libre

MAP U1 ■ Calle L & Av. 23, Vedado ■ 7834 6100 ■ www.meliacuba.com ■ $$$
The key attractions of this 1950s high-rise in the heart of Vedado include a bank, a leading nightclub, a business center, tour desks, and a pool. The refurbished rooms are comfortable and contemporary in style.

Meliá Cohiba

MAP S1 ■ Paseo at Av. 1ra, Vedado ■ 7833-3636 ■ www.meliacuba.com ■ $$$
The business hotel par excellence in Havana, this modern Spanish-run place has the best facilities in town, with deluxe rooms, excellent restaurants, and a vast swimming pool.

Town Center Hotels

Hotel Camino de Hierro, Camagüey
MAP L3 ■ Plaza de la Solidaridad ■ (32) 28 4264 ■ www.hoteles cubanacan.com ■ $$
A delightful newcomer in the heart of the historic district, this recently restored and rambling hotel has a graceful lobby and gourmet restaurant, and offers pleasantly furnished rooms with modern bathrooms.

Hotel Casa Granda, Santiago de Cuba
MAP P6 ■ Calle Heredia 201 ■ (22) 68 6600 ■ www.hoteles cubanacan.com ■ $$
This magnificent colonial-era hotel on the main square offers refurbished rooms with reproduction antique furniture and modern accoutrements. The restaurant offers gourmet cuisine, and the rooftop terrace bar offers great views and a lively social scene.

Hotel El Castillo, Baracoa
MAP R5 ■ Loma de Paraíso ■ (21) 64 5224 ■ www.gaviota-grupo. com ■ $$
The place to stay for postcard views of Baracoa and the unique El Yunque mountain (see p33), the rooms in this former fortress are comfortable and well-appointed with colonial furnishings. The restaurant is one of the best state-run options in town. A pool and tour desk are bonuses. It's only a two-minute walk into town, this involves a hike up and down a steep driveway or staircase.

Hotel E. Royalton, Bayamo
MAP N5 ■ Calle Maceo 53 ■ (23) 42 2290 ■ www. islazul.cu ■ $$
Built in the 1940s, this hotel is centrally located on the main square. The air-conditioned rooms, though not fancy, are comfortable, with TVs and clean bathrooms.

Hotel Gran, Camagüey
MAP L3 ■ Calle Maceo 67 ■ (32) 29 2093 ■ reserva@ granhotel.cmg.tur.cu ■ $$
This is a classic hotel that has been restored to its former grandeur. The top-floor restaurant has good views and serves excellent buffets. The nicely furnished, air-conditioned rooms offer safes, satellite TVs, and modern bathrooms.

Hotel Martí, Guantánamo
MAP Q5 ■ Calle Calixto García at Aguilera ■ (21) 32 9500 ■ $$
This hotel, which opened in 2012, stands next to Plaza Martí in the heart of town. It has modestly furnished rooms with modern bathrooms, and a pleasant restaurant.

Hotel del Rijo, Sancti Spíritus
MAP J3 ■ Calle Honorato del Castillo 12 ■ (41) 32 8588 ■ www.hoteles cubanacan.com ■ $$
A delightful colonial conversion on a charming plaza, this bargain-priced option has spacious, comfortable rooms with modern marble bathrooms. A good, hearty breakfast is provided, and there is an excellent restaurant.

Hotel San Basilio, Santiago de Cuba
MAP P6 ■ Calle San Basilio 403 ■ (22) 65 1702 ■ www.hoteles cubanacan.com ■ $$
An intimate and friendly hotel close to Parque Céspedes, this colonial mansion has a restaurant and 24-hour bar, plus a patio overlooking the square. The clean rooms are simple, with phones, safes, and TVs.

Hotel La Unión, Cienfuegos
MAP G3 ■ Calle 31 & Av. 54 ■ (43) 55 1020 ■ www.hoteles cubanacan.com ■ $$
Restored to its original 19th-century glory, Hotel Unión is the town's best. Its comfortable rooms surround a pretty court-yard with a fountain.

Hotel Vuelta Abajo, Pinar del Río
MAP B3 ■ Calle Martí 103 ■ (48) 75 9381 ■ $$
This small, colonial-era hotel with spacious, simply furnished rooms has a no-frills restaurant and bar, plus Internet service. Rooms with a balcony cost a little more. Its downtown location is handy, but street noise can be a nuisance.

Iberostar Gran Hotel Trinidad, Trinidad
MAP H4 ■ Calle Martí 262 ■ (41) 99 6070 ■ www. iberostar.com ■ $$$
This deluxe, inner-city hotel has a gleaming marble staircase leading to 45 luxurious rooms and a restaurant that is one of the finest outside Havana. Added draws include a billiards room and cigar lounge.

Rural Hotels

Hotel Hanabanilla, Sierra Escambra

MAP H3 ▪ Embalse Hanabanilla ▪ (42) 20 8461 ▪ recepcion@ hanabanilla.co.cu ▪ $

A stunning lakeside setting in the foothills of the Sierra Escambray make up for the dull architecture of this Soviet-inspired two-star hotel. Rooms are refurbished, with modern amenities. Local tours are offered. It can get noisy on weekends.

Motel La Belén, El Pilar

MAP L4 ▪ Comunidad El Pilar ▪ (52) 19 5744 ▪ ecotur@caonao.cu ▪ $

This off-the-beaten-track hotel in Sierra del Chorillo, southeast of Camagüey city, appeals to nature lovers. The five spacious rooms have modern bathrooms, and there is a cozy lounge as well as a swimming pool.

Villa Pinares de Mayarí, Pinares de Mayarí

MAP P5 ▪ Loma La Mensura ▪ (24) 45 5628 ▪ www.gaviota-grupo. com ▪ $

This charmingly Alpine-style mountain resort offers hiking, mountain biking, and bird-watching. Set amid pine forests near lakes and waterfalls, it can only be reached via a daunting unpaved road.

Horizontes Villa Soroa, Soroa

MAP C2 ▪ Carretera de Soroa, km 8 ▪ (48) 52 3534 ▪ www.hoteles cubanacan.com ▪ $$

Surrounded by forested hills, this bucolic option offers a lovely natural setting, with leafy grounds that slope down to a swimming pool. Choose from comfy cabins or spacious self-catering villas with private pools.

Hotel Las Jazmines, Viñales

MAP B2 ▪ Carretera a Viñales, km 23 ▪ (48) 79 6205 ▪ www.hoteles cubanacan.com ▪ $$

Housed in an original 1950s neo-colonial pink structure, this hotel has a spectacular hilltop setting that guarantees incredible views. Of the three room types available, the most comfortable are those in the modern annex.

Hotel La Moka, Las Terrazas

MAP C2 ▪ Autopista Habana-Pinar del Río, km 51 ▪ (48) 57 8602 ▪ www.lasterrazas.cu ▪ $$

Poised over Las Terrazas village and shrouded in woodland, this colonial-themed hotel focuses on ecotourism, with a lobby that is built around a tree. The spacious rooms offer scenic forest views.

Rancho Charco Azul, Artemisa

MAP D2 ▪ Cayajabos, 9 miles (14km) W of Artemisa ▪ 7649 1055 or 7204 5188 ▪ $$

A peaceful country retreat, this converted coralstone mansion is at the center of a horse-breeding facility and opened in 2016 as a eco-friendly boutique hotel with four rooms and eight chalets. Facilities include a swimming pool and dining, and horseback riding is offered.

Rancho San Vicente, Viñales

MAP B2 ▪ Carretera a Puerto Esperanza, km 33 ▪ (48) 79 6201 ▪ www. hotelescubanacan.com ▪ $$

This refuge in a wooded valley features simple air-conditioned cabins, with porches and huge windows. A lovely restaurant overlooks the pool.

Villa Cayo Saetía, Cayo Saetía

MAP P4 ▪ Cayo Saetía ▪ (24) 51 6900 ▪ www. gaviota-grupo.com ▪ $$

This beachside cabin complex is on a forested island once used for hunting by Communist officials, hence the abundance of exotic wildlife. The rustic restaurant is adorned with animal heads.

Villa Mirador de Mayabe, Mayabe

MAP N4 ▪ Alturas de Mayabe, km 8 ▪ (24) 42 2160 ▪ www.islazul.cu ▪ $$

Perched atop a hill with spectacular valley views, this villa has a clifftop pool and thatched restaurant popular with tour groups and locals. The refitted cabins have air-conditioning, satellite TVs, fridges, and telephones.

Villa El Saltón, El Saltón

MAP N5 ▪ Carretera Filé, Tercer Frente ▪ (22) 56 6326 ▪ www.campismo popular.cu ▪ $$

Focused on ecotourism, this riverside hotel, surrounded by forest, offers guided hikes and bird-watching trips. Rooms are simply furnished but have satellite TV. The restaurant overlooks a waterfall.

Villa San José del Lago, Yaguajay
MAP J2 ▪ Av. Antonio Guiteras ▪ (41) 54 6108 ▪ www.islazul.cu ▪ $$
On the north coast road of Sancti Spíritus province, this peaceful complex features deliciously warm thermal swimming pools and a lake with rowboats and flamingos. Air-conditioned cabins are simple yet comfy. Popular with Cubans, the place comes alive on weekends.

Beach Hotels

Iberostar Daiquirí, Cayo Guillermo
MAP K2 ▪ Ciego de Avila, Cayo Guillermo ▪ (33) 30 1712 ▪ www.ibero star.com ▪ $$
Modest in scale, this handsome 312-room all-inclusive resort is set in lush grounds and has a full range of watersports, plus excellent children's facilities. It offers cabaret and other themed shows in the evenings.

Villa Maguana, Playa Maguana
MAP R5 ▪ Baracoa–Moa road, km 20 ▪ (21) 64 1204 ▪ www.gavioto-grupo.com ▪ $$
Four rustic, two-story villas sit in dense foliage close to a private cove. Rooms are simple but comfortably furnished. Playa Maguana, a palm-fringed white-sand public beach, is close by.

Blau Marina Varadero, Varadero
MAP F2 ▪ Punta Hicacos, Autopista del Sur Final ▪ (45) 66 9966 ▪ www. blauhotels.com ▪ $$$
This deluxe all-inclusive resort has nautically

themed decor. Rooms feature state-of-the-art amenities, and the pool has a huge spiral water-slide. However, its location at the remote eastern tip of the peninsula is a long way from town.

Brisas Trinidad del Mar, Playa Ancón
MAP H4 ▪ Peninsula Ancón ▪ (41) 99 6500 ▪ www.hoteles cubanacan.com ▪ $$$
Architecture at this modern, Neo-Classical all-inclusive hotel integrates elements inspired by the colonial buildings of nearby Trinidad. Rooms have modern amenities.

Hotel Cayo Levisa, Pinar del Rio
MAP B3 ▪ Palma Rubia, La Palma ▪ (48) 75 6501 ▪ www.hotelescubana can.com ▪ $$$
This hotel, on the pristine island of Cayo Levisa, is accessed by boat from the mainland. It offers three types of beachfront accommodation, including fourplex wooden villas. Guests can enjoy activities such as diving and snorkeling in calm turquoise waters. The restaurant caters to day visitors as well as guests.

Iberostar, Ensenachos
MAP J1 ▪ Cayo Ensenachos, Cayos Villa Clara ▪ (42) 35 0300 ▪ www.iberostar.com ▪ $$$
This is one of Cuba's most luxurious all-inclusive resorts, spread out over miles of grounds; as a result, many rooms are a considerable walk from the beach. A highlight is the children's water park.

Mansión Xanadu, Varadero
MAP F2 ▪ Autopista del Sur, km 8.5 ▪ (45) 66 7388 ▪ www.varaderogolfclub. com ▪ $$$
In the former mansion of the DuPont family, this deluxe hotel has six huge, marble-floored rooms with private balconies, a fine restaurant, and an atmospheric bar with live music. Guests get golf privileges at the club.

Meliá Cayo Coco, Cayo Coco
MAP K2 ▪ Cayo Coco ▪ (33) 30 1180 ▪ www. meliacuba.com ▪ $$$
A chic all-inclusive that outshines other hotels on the island. It caters to adults only, and room options include two-story cabins overhanging a natural seawater lagoon. Guests have a choice of four restaurants.

Meliá Cayo Santa María, Cayo Santa María
MAP J1 ▪ (42) 35 0200 ▪ www.meliacuba.com ▪ $$$
Elegant and all-inclusive, with a vast pool complex, this hotel offers a choice of gourmet restaurants, lively entertainment, and plenty of water sports.

Meliá Marina Varadero, Varadero
MAP F2 ▪ Autopista del Sur y Final ▪ (45) 66 7330 ▪ www.meliacuba.com ▪ $$$
Near the far eastern end of the peninsula, this sensational luxury hotel overlooks Cuba's largest marina. It boasts beautiful rooms, multiple gourmet restaurants, and tranquil spa facilities.

For a key to hotel price categories see p128

Paradisus Río de Oro, Guardalavaca

MAP P4 ■ Playa Esmeralda ■ (24) 43 0090 ■ www.meliacuba.com ■ $$$

This huge yet friendly all-inclusive is built around a giant swimming pool. Facilities include multiple bars, and entertainment for adults and kids.

Sol Cayo Largo, Cayo Largo

MAP F4 ■ Playa Lindamar ■ (45) 24 8260 ■ www.meliacuba.com ■ $$$

A lovely all-inclusive resort on a spectacular stretch of white sand. Sol Cayo Largo has a pool and several restaurants. The rooms are painted in bright pastel colors.

Budget Hotels

Hotel Colón, Camagüey

MAP L3 ■ Av. República 472 ■ (32) 25 4878 ■ www.islazul.cu ■ $

A historic hotel opened in 1926, the restored Hotel Colón has a gleaming mahogany bar, which is a great place for cocktails, while the restaurant is considered one of the city's most elegant. One room is equipped for disabled travelers.

Hotel Rex, Santiago de Cuba

MAP P6 ■ Av. Garzón 10 ■ (22) 68 7233 ■ www.islazul.cu ■ $

This historic hotel, which has been refurbished in a modern fashion, offers great value for money. It has a stylish restaurant and bar and is the only hotel in Santiago de Cuba offering Wi-Fi across its entire premises.

Motel Punta Blanca, Varadero

MAP F2 ■ Av. Kawama Final ■ (45) 66 2410 ■ www.islazul.cu ■ $

Tucked away in the far west end of the peninsula, three private villas have been combined to form this budget boutique hotel. Punta Blanca is one of the best value options in Varadero.

Hotel Caribbean, La Habana Vieja

MAP V4 ■ Paseo de Martí 164 ■ 7860 8210 ■ www.islazul.cu ■ $$

This inexpensive hotel is conveniently located on Paseo de Martí in Centro Habana. The clean, air-conditioned rooms are in lively color schemes and have satellite TV. The ground-floor café opens onto the loud Paseo.

Hotel E. La Ronda, Trinidad

MAP H4 ■ Calle Martí 239 ■ (41) 99 8538 ■ www.hotelescubanacan.com ■ $$

A remodeled colonial town house on the edge of Parque Céspedes and the colonial quarter, it offers ample comfort in 14 air-conditioned rooms with mid-20th-century decor.

Hotel E. Velasco, Matanzas

MAP E2 ■ Calle Contreras 79 ■ (45) 25 3880 ■ www.hotelescubanacan.com ■ $$

The only hotel in Matanzas is set in a restored early 20th-century building on Parque Libertad. A small, boutique-style hotel, its rooms are attractively decorated. The restaurant is one of the better places to eat in town.

Hotel Mascotte, Remedios

MAP J2 ■ Calle Máximo Gómez 114 ■ (42) 39 5341 ■ www.hoteles cubanacan.com ■ $$

This renovated historic hotel is situated just off the main plaza. All 10 rooms have modern bathrooms, and the restaurant is one of the best in town.

Hotel Ordoño, Gibara

MAP P4 ■ Calle J. Peralta between Marmól & Independencia ■ (24) 84 4448 ■ www.hoteles cubanacan.com ■ $$

Occupying a colonial mansion in the center of town, which was recently restored, Ordoño features exquisite murals in its 21 rooms on two levels.

Hotel Terral, Centro Habana

MAP V1 ■ Malecón & Lealtad ■ www.haba guanex.cu ■ 7860 2100 ■ $$

Opened in 2012, this is a stylish contemporary hotel that overlooks the Malecón, and has 14 spacious rooms, complete with modern amenities.

Villa Las Brujas, Cayo Santa Maria

MAP J1 ■ Cayo Las Brujas ■ (42) 35 0025 ■ www.gaviota-grupo.com ■ $$

A smart yet rustic beach hotel, Villa Las Brujas is attractively laid out along a wooden walkway that runs from the marina to the beach. Many of the simply furnished wooden bungalows overlook the sea. Resort facilities include two Jacuzzis, a restaurant with sea views, and access to a narrow but long beach.

Villa Los Caneyes, Santa Clara

MAP H3 ▪ Av. de los Eucaliptos ▪ (42) 21 8140 ▪ www.hoteles cubanacan.com ▪ $$
Popular with tour groups, this hotel on the outskirts of town has comfortable, octagonal, thatched cabins with air conditioning and satellite TV. The elegant restaurant has buffet and à la carte meals. A poolside fashion show is held each evening.

Private Room Rentals

Casa Beny, Varadero

MAP F1 ▪ Calle 55 124 ▪ (45) 61 1700 ▪ www.benyhouse.com ▪ $
It was only in 2011 that private room rentals were legalized in Varadero. Of the many that popped up, Casa Beny stands out. It offers every comfort, plus delicious meals prepared by the attentive owners, a beautifully landscaped garden, and even parking.

Casa Caridad, Camagüey

MAP L3 ▪ Calle Oscar Primelles No. 310A ▪ (32) 29 1554 ▪ abreucmg@ enet.cu ▪ $
Run by a lovely hostess, this place has three identical bedrooms along a corridor that opens out into the family lounge, and a patio, where meals are served beneath an arbor.

Casa Colonial Maruchi, Santiago de Cuba

MAP P6 ▪ Calle Hartmann (San Félix) 357 ▪ (22) 62 0767 ▪ maruchib@ yahoo.es ▪ $
At one of the city's most professionally run casas

particulares, two guest rooms feature colonial-period furniture and share a bathroom; a third has a private terrace. A gorgeous basset hound roams the delightful central patio.

Casa Colonial Muñoz, Trinidad

MAP H4 ▪ Calle Martí 401 ▪ (41) 99 3673 ▪ www.casa.trinidadphoto.com
A spacious 18th-century home full of antiques is run by the knowledgeable and friendly Muñoz family, who speak English and can assist travelers. Each of the three bedrooms has a private bathroom. Delicious dinners are also served to guests.

Casa Font, Trinidad

MAP H4 ▪ Calle Gustavo Izquierdo 105 ▪ (41) 99 3683 ▪ www.casafont trinidad.jimdo.com ▪ $
This enormous 18th-century family home is stunningly furnished with beautiful Spanish colonial heirlooms. One of the rooms features an elegant bed decorated in mother-of-pearl. Friendly host Beatriz serves breakfast in the patio garden.

Casa de Jorge Coalla, Havana

MAP S1 ▪ Calle 1 456, Vedado ▪ 7832 9032 ▪ www.havanaroom rental.com ▪ $
A friendly family hosts visitors in this two-room casa particular superbly located in Vedado close to key sites and a good choice of restaurants. The spacious, air-conditioned rooms are well-equipped, and the bathrooms have lots of hot water.

Casa de Juan Sánchez, Cienfuegos

MAP G3 ▪ Av. 8 #3703 ▪ (43) 51 7986 ▪ casa juanche@nauta.cu ▪ $
Dramatic Modernist architecture is the appeal of this 1950s home in the Punta Gorda district. The single bedroom is cross-ventilated and has a well-kept bathroom.

Hostal del Ángel, La Habana Vieja

MAP W4 ▪ Calle Cuarteles 118 ▪ 7860 0771 ▪ www.pradocolonial.com ▪ $
This delightful, homely option occupies a restored colonial town house on the edge of La Habana Vieja. The period furnishings are a highlight, as are the balconies, and a spiral staircase leads to a library.

Hostal El Chalet, Remedios

MAP J2 ▪ Calle Brigadier González 29 ▪ (42) 39 6538 ▪ $
This well-maintained 1950s home very close to the main square has two bedrooms. The one upstairs has a lounge, large bathroom, and an independent entrance. The other room has a smaller bathroom.

Villa Liba, Holguín

MAP N4 ▪ Calle Maceo 46 ▪ (24) 42 3823 ▪ mariela yoga@cristal.hlg.sld.cu ▪ $
A short walk from both downtown and the Loma de Cruz, this 1950s house is owned by a well-educated, friendly couple. The two spacious guest rooms have period furnishings and are air-conditioned. Hearty meals are served on the patio. It has secure parking.

For a key to hotel price categories see p128

Index

Acknowledgments

Author

Christopher P. Baker is an award-winning travel writer and photographer specializing in the Caribbean and Central America. His feature articles have appeared in more than 200 publications worldwide. His many books include the literary travelog *Mi Moto Fidel: Motorcycling Through Castro's Cuba.*

Publishing Director Georgina Dee

Publisher Vivien Antwi

Design Director Phil Ormerod

Editorial Michelle Crane, Rebecca Flynn, Rachel Fox, Fay Franklin, Priyanka Kumar, Scarlett O'Hara, Sally Schafer, Sophie Wright

Design Richard Czapnik, Marisa Renzullo, Stuti Tiwari, Vinita Venugopal

Commissioned Photography Ian O'Leary, Rough Guides/Greg Roden, Tony Souter

Picture Research Susie Peachey, Ellen Root, Lucy Sienkowska, Oran Tarjan

Cartography Subhashree Bharti, Zafar-ul Islam Khan, Suresh Kumar, James Macdonald

DTP Jason Little, George Nimmo

Production Nancy-Jane Maun

Factchecker Matthew Norman

Proofreader Clare Peel

Indexer Hilary Bird

Picture Credits

The publisher would like to thank the following for their kind permission to reproduce their photographs:
(**Key:** a-above; b-below/bottom; c-centre; f-far; l-left; r-right; t-top)

123RF.com: Greta Gabaglio 19tl.

4Corners: Werner Bertsch 22-3; Reinhard Schmid 3tr, 118-9.

Alamy Stock Photo: Rubens Abboud 81clb; age fotostock/Alberto Carrera 12-3, /Juan Muñoz 50crb, /Toño Labra 51t, 100-1; Aurora Photos/Beth Wald 89t; Author's Image Ltd/Mickael David 111ca; RC (Rick) Bauer 45tr; Sean David Baylis 65tr; Jens Benninghofen 2tr, 34-5; Bildagentur-online/Schickert 7tr, 78bl, 96tr; John Birdsall 57tr; Blend Images/ Jeremy Woodhouse 11br, 28crb, 31bl, 32bl; blickwinkel/McPHOTO/SCO 98tl; Ian Bottle

39c; Nelly Boyd 55tl; John Cairns 97b; Cephas Picture Agency/Joris Luyten 81cra; Tristan Deschamps 115tr; Dov Makabaw Cuba 10crb, 60br, 66tl, 80tr, 106cla, 106crb; dpa picture alliance 52tl; Adam Eastland 79tl; epa european pressphoto agency b.v. 46ca; Everett Collection Historical 41tr; F1online digitale Bildagentur GmbH/ Austrophoto 112br; Kevin Foy 46tl; tim gartside travel 12crb, 77tr; Astrid Harrisson 16br; hemis.fr/Patrick Escudero 4b; Hemis.fr/ Patrick Frilet 99cr; Ruth Hofshi 26cla; imageBROKER/Egon Bömsch 72cla, /Peter Schickert 26bl; INSADCO Photography/Martin Plöb 96clb; J Marshall - Tribaleye Images 48tr, /World Illustrated 40tl; Vojko Kavcic 110ca; Konstantin Kulikov 84tl; Lazyllama 17cra; David Litschel 48bl; Annette Lozinski 80cl, 84cra; Alain Machet (1) 57cla; Jill Meyer 44cra; Ian Nellist 29bc; nobleIMAGES/Kate Noble 21tl; B. O'Kane 88crb; Anne-Marie Palmer 40cra, 73t; Sunshine Pics 104b, 105cla; Wolfi Poelzer 18bl, 38bl, 87cla; Premaphotos 53tl; Ageev Rostislav 108bl; Sagaphoto.com/Patrick Forget 85tl; Antony Souter 25crb, 47cl, 74b; Kumar Sriskandan 109cla; Torontonian 58t; TravelMuse 107bl; Universal Images Group/DeAgostini/W. Buss 10cla; Westend61 GmbH/JLPfeifer 63tr; Westermann 49tr; Poelzer Wolfgang 4crb, 24crb, 82-3, 88cla.

Bridgeman Images: 43tl; Bibliotheque Nationale, Paris, France 36b, /Archives Charmet 37br.

Corbis: Atlantide Phototravel/Vittorio Sciosia 4cla; Walter Bibikow 66br; Phil Clarke Hill 67tr; Phil Clarke-Hill 49cl, 49bl; Destinations 63tl; epa/ Alejandro Ernesto 69cl, 69tr; the food passionates/ Eva Gründemann 62cb; Patrick Frilet 3tl, 70-1; Wael Hamzeh 59tr; Hemis/Patrick Frilet 60t, 75cl; imageBROKER/ GTW 92cla, / Hans Blossey 17tl; JAI/Walter Bibikow 4t, 65br; Frank Lukasseck 74cra; Pete Oxford 104tl; Radius Images 62br; Bernard Radvaner 107tr; Jose Fuste Raga 103cr; Reuters/Enrique de la Osa 68tr; Robert Harding Picture Library/Donald Nausbaum 61tr, /Michael DeFreitas 53br; Rachel Royse 64tr; Paul Starosta 32tl; Greg Stott 53clb; Jane Sweeney 94clb; Rodrigo Torres 93tl; Vittorio Sciosia 61clb, 65cl.

Dreamstime.com: Ansud 11crb, 28cla; Marcel Berendsen 11cr, 112t; Kian Yung Chua 20-1; Filipe Frazao 10tr, 14-5; Roxana González 47tr; Gudmund1 1, 54clb; Johann Helgason 90bl, Pablo Hidalgo 11cla, 26-7, Jedynakanna 7tl, 56tl; Juliorivalta 45bl; Kmiragaya 4cl, 16cl, 42b, 58c, 64bl, 85br; Konstik 16-7; Amanda Lewis 77cb; Marco Lijoi 29tl; Daniel Loncarevic 76b; Maisna 67cla; Roberto Machado Noa 103tl; Nobohh 44t; Palino666 86bl; Natalia Pavlova 10clb; Carlos Perez 4clb; Richard Semik 6cl, 11tr, 32-3; Dubes Sonego Junior 39tr; Nadezda Stoyanova 58bl; Rudolf Tepfenhart 10br; Aleksandar Todorovic 12bl, 14bl, 20br, 30cla, 55b, 111br, 113cla; Toniflap 2tl, 8-9; Tupungato 44bl; Sergey Uryadnikov 18cl, 24cla, 90cra, 98clb; Venemama 50cla; Visualife 33tl; Wafuefotodesign 52br; John Ward 33bl, 86tr.

Getty Images: AFP/Adalberto Roque 27bc; Ulf Andersen 42tl; Günter Nindl 59cl; PHAS/UIG 36tr; Rolls Press/Popperfoto 37cla; Jane Sweeney 30clb.

© Meliá Cuba Marketing & Publicity: 24-5.

Photoshot: World Pictures/Mel Longhurst 31cra.

Rex by Shutterstock: Associated Newspapers 43br; Patrick Frilet 112clb; Joaquin Hernandez 68b; imageBROKER 94l; Sovfoto/Universal Images Group 40bl; Underwood Archives/UIG 41clb.

Robert Harding Picture Library: Walter Bibikow 46br; Gunter Gruner 116t; Christopher Kimmel 24bl; Tono Labra 13tl; Martin Moxter 102tl; Juan Munoz 19cb; Ben Pipe 12cla; Alexander Poschel 21br; Ellen Rooney 15cr; Michael Runkel 30-1; Karl F. Schofmann 4cra, 14cla; Jane Sweeney 20cl; Therin-Weise 18-9.

Cover
Front and spine: **4Corners:** Reinhard Schmid.

Back: **Dreamstime.com:** Justek16.

Pull Out Map Cover
4Corners: Reinhard Schmid.

All other images © Dorling Kindersley
For further information see:
www.dkimages.com

As a guide to abbreviations in visitor information blocks: **Adm** = *admission charge;* **DA** = *disabled access;* **D** = *dinner;* **L** = *lunch.*

Penguin Random House

Printed and bound in China

First American Edition, 2008
Published in the United States by DK Publishing, 345 Hudson Street, New York, New York 10014

Copyright 2008, 2017 © Dorling Kindersley Limited

A Penguin Random House Company

16 17 18 19 10 9 8 7 6 5 4 3 2 1

Reprinted with revisions 2010, 2012, 2014, 2017

Published in Great Britain by Dorling Kindersley Limited.

A catalog record for this book is available from the Library of Congress.

ISSN 1479-344X
ISBN 978 1 4654 5707 3

MIX
Paper from responsible sources
FSC™ C018179
www.fsc.org

SPECIAL EDITIONS OF DK TRAVEL GUIDES

DK Travel Guides can be purchased in bulk quantities at discounted prices for use in promotions or as premiums. We are also able to offer special editions and personalized jackets, corporate imprints, and excerpts from all of our books, tailored specifically to meet your own needs.

To find out more, please contact:

in the US
specialsales@dk.com

in the UK
travelguides@uk.dk.com

in Canada
specialmarkets@dk.com

in Australia
penguincorporatesales@ penguinrandomhouse.com.au

Phrase Book

The Spanish spoken in Cuba is basically the same as the Castilian used in Spain with certain deviations. As in the Spanish-speaking countries in Central and Southern America, the "z" is pronounced like the "s", as is the "c" when it comes before "e" and "i". Among the grammatical variations, visitors should be aware that Cubans use *Ustedes* in place of *Vosotros*, to say "you" when referring to more than one person. It is notable that some Indian, African, and English words are commonly used in present-day Cuban Spanish. This basic phrase book includes useful common phrases and words, and particular attention has been paid to typically Cuban idioms in a list of Cuban Terms.

Emergencies

Help!	¡Socorro!	sokorro
Stop!	¡pare!	pareh
Call a doctor	Llamen a un médico	yamen a oon medeeko
Call an ambulance	Llamen a una ambulancia	yamen a oona amboolans-ya
Police!	¡Policía!	poleesee-a
I've been robbed	Me robaron	meh robaron

Communication Essentials

Yes	Sí	see
No	No	no
Please	Por favor	por fabor
Pardon me	Perdone	pairdoneh
Excuse me	Disculpe	deeskoolpeh
I'm sorry	lo siento	lo s-yento
Thanks	Gracias	gras-yas
Hello!	¡Buenas!	bwenas
Good day	Buenos días	bwenos dee-as
Good afternoon	Buenas tardes	bwenas tardes
Good evening	Buenas noches	bwenas noches
night	noche	nocheh
morning	mañana	man-yana
tomorrow	mañana	man-yana
yesterday	ayer	a-yair
Here	Acá	aka
How?	¿Cómo?	komo
When?	¿Cuándo?	kwando
Where?	¿Dónde?	dondeh
Why?	¿Por qué?	por keh
How are you?	¿Qué tal?	keh tal
It's a pleasure!	¡Mucho gusto!	moocho goosto
Goodbye	Hasta luego	asta lwego

Useful Phrases

That's fine	Está bien/ocá	esta b-yen/oka
Fine	¡Qué bien!	keh b-yen
How long?	¿Cuánto falta?	kwanto falta
Do you speak a little English?	¿Habla un poco de inglés?	abla oon poko deh eengles
I don't understand	No entiendo	no ent-yendo
Could you speak more slowly?	¿Puede hablar más despacio?	pwedeh ablas mas despas-yo
I agree/ OK	De acuerdo/ Ocá	deh akwairdo/ oka
Certainly!	¡Claro que sí!	klaro keh see!
Let's go!	¡Vámonos!	bamonos

Useful Words

large	grande	grandeh
small	pequeño	peken-yo
hot	caliente	kal-yenteh
cold	frío	free-o
good	bueno	bweno
bad	malo	malo
well/fine	bien	b-yen
open	abierto	ab-yairto
closed	cerrado	serrado
full	lleno	yeno
empty	vacío	basee-o
right	derecha	dairecha
left	izquierda	isk-yairda
straight	recto	rekto
under	debajo	debaho
over	arriba	arreeba
quickly/ early	pronto/ temprano	pronto/ temprano
late	tarde	tardeh
now	ahora	a-ora
delay	demorra	deh-morra
more	más	mas
less	menos	menos
little	poco	poko
sufficient	suficiente	soofees-yenteh
much	mucho/muy	moocho/mwee
too much	demasiado	demas-yado
in front of	delante	delanteh
behind	detrás	detras
first floor	primer piso	preemair peeso
ground floor	planta baja	planta baha
lift/elevator	elevador	elebador
bathroom/toilet	servicios baños	sairbees-yos ban-yos
women	mujeres	moohaires
men	hombres	ombres
toilet paper	papel sanitario	papel saneetar-yo
camera	cámara	kamara
batteries	baterías	batairee-as
passport	pasaporte	pasaporteh
visa; tourist card	visa; tarjeta turistica	beesa; tarheta tooreesteeka

Transport

Could you call a taxi for me?	¿Me puede llamar a un taxi?	meh pwedeh yamar a oon taksee?
airport	aeropuerto	a-airopwairto
train station	estación de ferrocarriles	estas-yon deh fairrokarreeles
bus station	terminal de guagua	tairmeenal deh gwa-gwa
When does it leave?	¿A qué hora sale?	a keh ora saleh?
customs	aduana	adwana
boarding pass	tarjeta de embarque	tarheta deh embarkeh
car hire	alquiler de carros	alkeelair deh karros
bicycle	bicicleta	beeseekleta
insurance	seguro	segooro
petrol/gas station	estación de gasolina	estas-yon deh gasoleena

Staying in a Hotel

single room/ double	habitación sencilla/ doble	abeetas-yon sensee-ya /dobleh
shower	ducha	doocha
bathtub	bañera	ban-yaira
balcony	balcón, terraza	balkon, tairrasa
warm water	agua caliente	agwa kal-yenteh
cold water	agua fría	agwa free-a
soap	jabón	habon
towel	toalla	to-a-ya
key	llave	yabeh

Eating Out

What is there to eat?	¿Qué hay para comer?	keh I para komair?
The bill please	La cuenta por favor	la kwenta por fabor
I would like some water	Quisiera un poco de agua	kees-yaira oon poko deh agwa
Do you have wine?	¿Tienen vino?	t-yenen beeno?
The beer is not cold enough	La cerveza no está bien fría	la sairbesa no esta b-yen free-a
breakfast	desayuno	desa-yoono
lunch	almuerzo	almwairso
dinner	comida	komeeda
raw/cooked	crudo/cocido	kroodo/koseedo
glass	vaso	baso
cutlery	cubiertos	koob-yairtos

Menu Decoder

aceite	asayteh	oil
agua mineral	agwa meenairal	mineral water
aguacate	agwakateh	avocado
ajo	aho	garlic
arroz	urros	rice
asado	asado	roasted
atún	atoon	tuna
azúcar	asookar	sugar
bacalao	bakala-o	cod
café	kafeh	coffee
camarones	kamarones	prawns
carne	karneh	meat
cerveza	sairbesa	beer
congrí	kongree	rice with beans and onions
dulce	doolseh	sweet, dessert
ensalada	ensalada	salad
fruta	froota	fruit
fruta bomba	froota bomba	papaya
helado	elado	ice cream
huevo	webo	egg
jugo	hoogo	fruit juice
langosta	langosta	lobster
leche	lecheh	milk
mantequilla	mantekee-ya	butter
marisco	mareesko	seafood
pan	pan	bread
papas	papas	potatoes
pescado	peskado	fish
plátano	platano	banana
pollo	po-yo	chicken
postre	postreh	dessert

potaje/sopa	potaheh/sopa	soup
puerco cerdo	pwairko serrdo	pork
queso	keso	cheese
refresco	refresko	drink
sal	sal	salt
salsa	salsa	sauce
té	teh	tea
vinagre	beenagreh	vinegar

Cuban Terms

apagón	apagon	black-out, power outage
babalawo	babala-wo	a priest of Afro-Cuban religion
batey	batay	village around sugar factory
carro	karro	car
casa de la trova	kasa deh la troba	traditional music venue
cayo	ka-yo	small island
chama	chama	child
criollo	kr-yo-yo	Creole (born in Cuba of Spanish descent)
divisas	deebeesas	CUC (Cuban Convertible Peso)
chavitos	chabeetos	CUC (slang)
eva	eba	woman
guagua	gwagwa	bus
guajiro	gwaheero	farmer
guarapo	gwarapo	sugar cane juice
ingenio	eenhen-yo	sugar factory complex
jama	hama	food, meal
jinetera	heenetaira	prostitute, or female hustler
jinetero	heenetairo	male person hustling tourists
libreta	leebreta	rations book
moneda nacional	moneda nas-yonal	pesos ("national currency")
moros y cristianos	moros ee krist-yanos	rice and black beans
paladar	paladar	privately owned restaurant
puro	pooro	authentic Cuban cigar
santero	santairo	santería priest
tabaco	tabako	low-quality cigar
tienda	t-yenda	shop that only accepts CUC
trago	trago	alcoholic drink
tunas	toonas	prickly pears
zafra	safra	sugarcane harvest

Health

I don't feel well	Me siento mal	meh s-yento mal
I have a...	Me duele...	meh dweleh...
stomach ache	el estómago	el estomago
headache	la cabeza	lu kabesa
He/she is ill	Está enfermo/a	esta enfairmo
I need to rest	Necesito decansar	neseseeto dekansar
drug store	farmacia	farmasee-ya

Post Office and Bank

bank	*banco*	*banko*
I want to send a letter	*Quiero enviar una carta*	*k-yairo emb-yar oona karta*
postcard	*postal tarjeta*	*postal tarheta*
stamp	*sello*	*se-yo*
draw out money	*sacar dinero*	*sakar deenairo*

Shopping

How much is it?	*¿Cuánto cuesta?*	*kwanto kwesta*
What time do you open/close?	*¿A qué hora abre/cierra?*	*a ke ora abreh/s-yairra*
May I pay with a credit card?	*¿Puedo pagar con tarjeta de crédito?*	*pwedo pagar kon tarheta deh kredeeto?*

Sightseeing

beach	*playa*	*pla-ya*
castle, fortress	*castillo*	*kastee-yo*
cathedral	*catedral*	*katedral*
church	*iglesia*	*eegles-ya*
district	*barrio*	*barr-yo*
garden	*jardín*	*hardeen*
guide	*guía*	*gee-a*
house	*casa*	*kasa*
motorway	*autopista*	*owtopeesta*
museum	*museo*	*mooseh-o*
park	*parque*	*parkeh*
road	*carretera*	*karretaira*
square, plaza	*plaza, parque*	*plasa, parkeh*
street	*calle, callejón*	*ka-ye, ka-yehon*
town hall	*Ayuntamiento*	*a-yoontam-yento*
tourist bureau	*buró de turismo*	*booro deh tooreesmo*

Numbers

0	*cero*	*sairo*
1	*uno*	*oono*
2	*dos*	*dos*
3	*tres*	*tres*
4	*cuatro*	*kuatro*
5	*cinco*	*seenko*
6	*seis*	*says*
7	*siete*	*s-yeteh*
8	*ocho*	*ocho*
9	*nueve*	*nwebeh*
10	*diez*	*d-yes*
11	*once*	*onseh*
12	*doce*	*doseh*
13	*trece*	*treseh*
14	*catorce*	*katorseh*
15	*quince*	*keenseh*
16	*dieciséis*	*d-yeseesays*
17	*diecisiete*	*d-yesees-yeteh*
18	*dieciocho*	*d-yesee-yocho*
19	*diecinueve*	*d-yeseenwebeh*
20	*veinte*	*baynteh*
30	*treinta*	*traynta*
40	*cuarenta*	*kwarenta*
50	*cincuenta*	*seenkwenta*
60	*sesenta*	*sesenta*
70	*setenta*	*setenta*
80	*ochenta*	*ochenta*
90	*noventa*	*nobenta*
100	*cien*	*s-yen*

Time

minute	*minuto*	*meenooto*
hour	*hora*	*ora*
half-hour	*media hora*	*med-ya ora*
Monday	*lunes*	*loones*
Tuesday	*martes*	*martes*
Wednesday	*miércoles*	*m-yairkoles*
Thursday	*jueves*	*hwebes*
Friday	*viernes*	*b-yairnes*
Saturday	*sábado*	*sabado*
Sunday	*domingo*	*domeengo*
January	*enero*	*enairo*
February	*febrero*	*febrairo*
March	*marzo*	*marso*
April	*abril*	*abreel*
May	*mayo*	*ma-yo*
June	*junio*	*hoon-yo*
July	*julio*	*hool-yo*
August	*agosto*	*agosto*
September	*septiembre*	*sept-yembreh*
October	*octubre*	*oktoobreh*
November	*noviembre*	*nob-yembreh*
December	*diciembre*	*dees-yembreh*